DRAW
A BETTER
BUSINESS

the essential visual thinking
toolkit to help your small
business work better

First published in Great Britain by Practical Inspiration Publishing, 2018

Layout design by www.lineanddotcreative.com

The moral rights of the author have been asserted

ISBN 978-1-910056-63-9

See more of our work at

www.graphicchange.com

for natasha

The famous French architect Le Corbusier once said, "I prefer drawing to talking. Drawing is faster and leaves less room for lies." Le Corbusier would have loved Cara's wonderful book. It is fast to digest, beautiful on the eyes, and full of deep truth. Whether you're a businessperson looking to clarify your vision, or a creative person looking to make sense of business, this book is a gem.

Dan Roam — author of *The Back of the Napkin* and *Draw to Win*

In *Draw a Better Business*, Cara Holland provides a visual working toolkit that will help clarify your entrepreneurial plans and then enhance dialogue you have with customers, staff, suppliers, investors and most importantly with yourself!

Andrew Greenman — Assistant Professor, Entrepreneurship and Small Business, Nottingham University Business School

There's hardly a soul who wouldn't benefit from the ideas in Cara's book.

Tea Uglow — Creative Director, Google's Creative Lab, Sydney

This powerful and practical book will transform your business. Grab a pen and supercharge your communication with Cara as your guide to build your confidence, skills, and impact through drawing.

Bec Evans — co-founder of Prolifiko

In the competitive world of consulting, it's priceless to acquire skills that immediately improve business. Cara is a NINJA! After starting to use these tools, I'm seeing massive benefits with clients already!

Madelyn Gengelbach — Principal, Market Tuning Group

Often, business people don't think of themselves as creative; however, Cara's book shows the 'non-artist' how to use visual communication tools to create and capture innovative solutions that will engage your audience and transform your business.

Melanie Eusebe — Consultant, Professor, Founder of Black British Business Awards

contents

part 1

....

1
introduction   **17**

who is this book for?
how does this book work?

2
work visually   **31**

what is visual thinking and working
visually all about?
seeing
thinking
drawing
equipment

3
why?   **45**

you're designed to be visual
it's more engaging
it's quicker
it's more effective
it's stickier
it's more inclusive
it's helpful
it's good for you
interview with Jen Harvey

part 2

part 3

"there can be no words without images"

Aristotle

foreword

If you're an entrepreneur or small-business owner and you've ever wondered if visual thinking was something that could work for you — not just for big businesses — then the answer is definitely "Yes".

Visual thinking has contributed in some way to every success I've had in life, from the businesses I've founded, to family, to personal discipline and even to my health.

Visual thinking quite literally makes you see better. It enables you to come up with creative solutions that you wouldn't otherwise arrive at, helps you make sense of complex systems and see connections that others miss. It not only helps you explain this complexity to your clients, it helps them see the answers to their problems. Most businesses are made up of people walking around with problems that they are trying to fix using an incomplete toolkit. Their solutions often fail because they are missing the wealth of information that visual thinking can unlock. Put simply, visual thinking helps you get better at seeing so that you can get better at fixing.

This works in pretty much any situation. I've never been super strong at math, but even my math is better when I work visually.

I'm thrilled to recommend this book, **Draw a Better Business** by **Cara Holland**. It's extremely simple, clear, actionable, and of course it's got lots of pictures so it's pretty easy to navigate. I think it's a wonderful book and I hope you enjoy it.

Dave Gray — Founder, XPLANE
Founder and CEO, The School of the Possible 2018

whether you want
to connect with an
individual, an audience
or the whole world,
communicating visually
helps you connect
more directly, and more
meaningfully, with more
people.

my mission is to help people draw their stories, conversations and ideas. to externalise the imagination and clarify the complex. to connect. because when we connect amazing things become possible.

part

we are living in
exciting times

1

introduction

Just a bit easier

Recently I was training a group of executives how to work visually. Nothing new about that, except the group was based in New Delhi and I was in Nottingham in the UK, being live streamed into their training room. As a child, this was the stuff of science fiction.

The future is here, and this brings with it a whole heap of new things to think about. We have never been more connected or more exposed to innovation and developments taking place around the globe.

We want the businesses we buy from and the people we work with to do better, to be better; we want to see innovation, empathy and human-centred design in everything, from the jeans we wear to the coffee we drink.

We are dealing with mega shifts in employment trends. Between huge tech advancements and the increase in gig working, the World Economic Forum predicts that creativity and creative problem solving are the top skills we will need in the future.[1]

So it's no surprise that as entrepreneurs and small business owners it can feel like a tough ask to keep up. How do we make our business more collaborative in its approach? More creative and innovative in its delivery?

I don't have a magic wand, but what if I told you there are ways to make it just that bit easier? That there is a way of working that can help you really work in a new way, and that you can use these skills to run a business that is better? Better for you and better for your clients?

Welcome to the world of working visually. In this book I'm going to teach you some new skills, share some ideas and hopefully give you the knowledge you need to start working differently. To start working visually.

Now, I'm not talking here about working as a 'creative', but I am talking about working more creatively. Using visual thinking skills and tools to deliver your existing work more effectively, whatever type of business you run.

This is a **PLUS** sum:

**Your existing business knowledge and methods
+ visual thinking skills and tools**

= business advantage

knowledge + method + visual thinking

= business advantage

I hope this book will help you see the world and see your business through a new lens. This book will give you skills and knowledge that will enhance your business and help you meet the demands of the modern customer, confident that as a visual worker, you're bringing something collaborative and engaging to the table.

In this book I'm going to share my knowledge and experience of working visually with big and small businesses, and of starting and running my own small business. This book is a toolkit that you can use from two perspectives:

inside your business

- It will help you **LOOK** in a new way, both at the internal workings of your business and externally to the context your business is operating within.

- It will help you **MAKE SENSE** of what you are doing and why it is, or isn't, working.

- It will help you **REFRAME** situations, challenges and questions that come up for you, helping you take new paths and arrive at new solutions.

externally with your clients

- It will help you **SHARE** your knowledge and your vision with others. With your clients, with your fans and with your bank manager.

- It will give you new tools and methods to **USE** with your clients.

- And finally, your new skills will enhance your ability to **THINK** in new, innovative ways throughout your business.

We're going to work together to focus on four key aspects of your business, each critical to your business success.

you

The most important part of your business. I'm going to give you the skills, confidence and know-how to start using visual tools. It doesn't matter what your drawing skills are, I'll teach you all the skills and tricks you need to start getting the benefits of working visually in your business.

planning

Whether your business is over a decade old like mine, or you're in the first quarter of your first year, you need to understand your own business journey in order to effectively plan a way forward. I'll share with you some great visual planning tools you can try out straight away.

engagement

When you're busy delivering, it can be easy to overlook the inner workings of what you do and how you do it. If you want to engage more clients or engage more effectively with the ones you've already got, then your business needs your time and attention as much as your clients do.

delivery

Finally, you're going to focus on your delivery. No more dusty flipcharts or death by slide deck. I'll show you tools and tricks that can transform your meetings and workshops into opportunities to create impactful and memorable connections.

I will give you tools to help you unleash your innate creativity, and by incorporating visual thinking and practice into your business, take your work to the next level.

This book is **PRACTICAL**, providing you with hands-on activities and techniques to try out inside your business, and with your clients. I want this book to **INSPIRE** and **ENERGISE** you, so that you can draw a better business and head back out into the world with a smile on your face and a marker pen in your hand.

i'm more comfortable with pictures than with words

I struggled at school. Not because I couldn't do the work, but because I wasn't a great fit with the system wrapped around the learning. I was a moody goth and I spent my fair share of time outside the deputy head's office. The exception was art class, where I could be found drawing moody, gothy things, with focus, and a huge desire to learn and do well.

In art class I was okay.

Years later, as a social worker, I discovered that working visually had the power to make it 'okay' for other people. It was a leveller. It encouraged participation in difficult conversations and made complex information-giving easier. It bridged a gap between me and a homeless teenager in a way that words just couldn't. When I started managing teams, I brought this learning with me. We drew our annual plans and I used pictures to explain funding cycles and to facilitate events.

By 2006 I was ready to start my own business, bringing what I'd learnt about working visually to other people. Since that day I've worked with household names like TimeWarner, Microsoft, Sony and Google. I've been party to discussions with business leaders, ministers and royalty, and I've drawn everywhere from a muddy field to Buckingham Palace.

As you can imagine, along the way I've learnt a lot of lessons. My aim is to help you draw yourself a better business, and have a whole new range of go-to methods in your toolkit.

I'm not a scientist or a professor, but I am a hands-on expert. I've put in my 10,000 hours and then some, and along the way I've learnt a **LOT**. Those lessons are what I want to share with you.

who is this book for?

Whether you're a start-up, an entrepreneur, a consultant or a small-business owner then this book is for you. You might be at the beginning of your business journey, or well on your way. If...

- you have a creative soul, even if you're not sure you have the creative talent to match

- spreadsheets and flipcharts hurt your brain or bore you to tears

- you've stopped developing your business in favour of 'doing' your business

- you want to work in creative, collaborative and effective ways with your clients

...then this book is for you.

You're not going to believe me yet, but you don't need to be artistic to use this book. Trust me. It's true.

it's about working visually, not creating art

It doesn't matter what kind of business you're running, or what your experience is of working creatively. **Draw a Better Business** is for everyone who wants to get their visual thinking brain in gear and get the business benefits.

how does this book work?

This book is designed to get you started working visually in your business.

If you like a bit of order then by all means work through the book from beginning to end. It was written in a logical order, but if the very thought of that makes you yawn, know that the book is designed so that you can dip in (and out!) as often as you like. **Draw a Better Business** is a resource you can keep coming back to again and again.

Here is the low-down on the sections in case you want to jump around:

part 1- working visually

This is a quick introduction to what we mean by visual thinking and working visually. Before diving in anywhere else, I recommend you read **chapter 2**, which explains why working visually is so powerful.

part 2 - you

This part of the book is focussed on **YOU**. We're going to turn you into a confident visual worker, so **chapter 5** is a 'drawing 101' boot camp, whilst **chapter 6** gives you more inspirational ideas for building your visual muscle memory with some daily habits. If you're already a confident drawer, you can jump to **part 3**.

part 3 - the toolkit

Now you're skilled up, let's give you some visual tools to use in your business. **Chapter 8** focuses on planning tools you can use on your own business but also with others (if you're a consultant, for example). **Chapter 9** is full of tools for customer and client engagement as well as tools to help you think about your business differently. Finally, **chapter 10** focuses on tools for delivery: think hacks for your flipcharts and meetings that really work hard for you.

All the tools and methods in this book are ones that you can use inside your business to improve your everyday, and externally to enhance your work with clients. I've put all the templates in a free workbook you can download as a reference tool at **graphicchange.com**.

If you like company when you're learning (and let's face it, working for yourself can be a lonely business) you can also hook up with us on social media **@graphicchange** using our hashtag **#DrawaBetterBusiness** and share your visual adventures, experiments and triumphs. I'll be there waiting to see how you're doing and cheering you on.

If you then head over to the Graphic Change Academy you'll find more free resources and our newsletter The Visual Edit.

If you know you want to apply these skills in your business but think you want more support, then you can access **Draw a Better Business** coaching over at **graphicchange.com** too.

Let's face it, we all have busy lives, with work, family and friends to juggle. But, and it's a big **BUT**, we also want to continue to learn, to improve our business and become the very best we can be. You've already made a commitment to the development of you and your business by buying this book, and that is a seriously great start.

you've got this!

"let the meaning of your work be obvious unless it is designed purely for your own amusement"

Edward Johnston

2

work
visually

what is visual thinking and working visually all about?

It's possible working visually might not mean exactly what you think it does. Sure, it involves some drawing, but it's not about making art or drawing pretty pictures. In fact, it doesn't always involve drawing pictures at all. Sometimes, a line, a box or an arrow is all you need.

Often, working visually involves a lot of sticky notes and marker pens. It's sometimes messy and usually fun, but it isn't about creativity for the sake of it. Working visually is about using your brain in a different way, enabling you to approach challenges, create solutions and engage others more effectively.

All of the exercises in this book are designed to get you **SEEING** differently, tuning in to the world of visual communication that is all around you. **THINKING** differently, harnessing your visual thinking skills throughout your business, and working differently, building your muscle memory for **DRAWING**, so that getting things out of your head and onto paper becomes second nature for you.

seeing

Imagine you're going on a journey, leaving from your front door and heading out to a supermarket. Now imagine you're making the journey in a world that doesn't rely on visual communication. No Google Maps, no satnav, no road signs, no black-and-white striped crossing, no red and green traffic lights, no shop sign, no big orange sales stickers showing you where the bargains are, no pictures of food on the packets, no logos... you get my point.

The world would be much harder to navigate without all of the visual clues we rely on. Visual clues that the majority of sighted people don't usually pay that much conscious attention to at all.

It's not our fault. It can be hard to focus when we're busy. Our minds are cluttered, our thoughts are turned inwards trying to work through the muddle, sometimes our conscious mind stops engaging entirely and we operate on auto pilot, not really aware of our surroundings at all.

So it's understandable that we don't always pay attention to all of the visual communication out there in the world.

But we do communicate visually all of the time by using colour, shape, scale, pictures and text in different ways. I want you to start building your visual muscle memory, consciously using your visual brain, and a good place to start is to start paying attention to what you see around you every day.

think about a post box

In the UK they are typically **RED** in colour and they are often an eye-catching shape. They usually stand alone, often towards the kerbside of the pavement where they are easy to spot.

They have a white rectangular sticker with the collection times in black, bold enlarged text, and the sticker is usually displayed in the same place; centrally placed below the letter slot. All of these decisions, used consistently, help us visually identify a letter box when we pass it. The Royal Mail is visually communicating with us, to help and encourage us to post letters. I'm sure this also applies if you don't live in the UK — post boxes the world over tend to be distinctive and uniform within a country.

Once you've started to pay attention to the visual clues around you, take it one step further. I want you to start to identify visuals that are trying to get us to behave in a certain way or are trying to help us understand how something works.

Think about a fire exit sign. In the UK they are often green and use the words **FIRE-EXIT** alongside a simple picture of a person exiting a door, or a directional arrow. All of the elements:

colour + words + image

combine to give us a clear and easy-to-understand message.

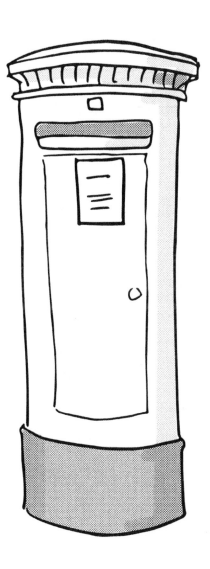

treasure hunt

Grab your camera or phone and have a wander around your home, your office, or outside in your community.

Keep a look out for visual communications: instructions, messages, directions or simple announcements that use visuals (sometimes with words alongside) to communicate.

Now in this exercise I'm not looking for logos that represent a brand, but for images or icons that are trying to communicate, inform or instruct us.

Once you start looking you'll see they are everywhere. On the cereal packet, on the coffee machine, on the fire extinguisher, on the USB cable, outside on the utility boxes and telegraph poles on your street.

Take photos of the ones that you find effective.

Start to notice all the forms of visual communication around you every day, and when you see a good example take a snap of it. What makes some more effective than others? Is it the image they've used? The words? The colour?

Also, and perhaps more importantly, have a think about what makes some not work as successfully.

thinking

Visual thinking means using images, shapes and colour, along with text, to help you think, process and communicate more effectively.

Let me give you an example. I recently spent a day with Hollywood screenwriting consultant, Bobette Buster.[2] She talked me through some story-telling universal truths script writers use.

I loved the idea of visualizing them to help people better understand their own storyline.

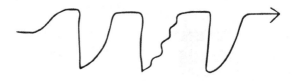

I met with Emma, who was a consultant and had spent three years delivering a multi-million project for a global client. She didn't want to head into another project, but was anxious about changing direction. I asked Emma to tell me her story. As we talked, I visually captured the plateaus, the times of free-fall such as redundancy, and the periods in the wilderness where she had, in the past, successfully worked out what to do next.

By the end, Emma felt confident about her ability to change direction, and to map out her next steps.

The conversation we had was important, but it was the visual that helped Emma's brain make the connections and have those "aha" moments.

after the session she said,
"Wow. I thought I knew everything
there was to know about my own
story, but seeing it drawn out
helped me notice patterns I just
hadn't been aware of, and that
was unexpectedly powerful."

visual thinking is powerful

As well as spotting patterns and making connections, working visually can help you:

- [ ] generate more ideas
- [ ] think more expansively (non-linear)
- [ ] retain information for longer
- [ ] understand information more fully
- [ ] get clarity from complexity
- [ ] recall content more fully
- [ ] solve problems
- [ ] communicate more effectively
- [ ] increase engagement / buy-in
- [ ] increase compliance

Working visually gives you some serious cognitive assistance. I'm not going to tell you how to think, because that would be weird. What I hope though, is that as you engage your visual thinking brain and use the skills in this book, you'll start to see the benefits for yourself.

drawing

The whole of the next section focuses on drawing, so I'm not going to say much more at this point, except this: you can draw, but if you're feeling doubtful, don't worry, I get it. For now, just trust me when I tell you that by the end of this book you'll be drawing yourself solutions, plans and ideas that are going to help your business. Remember I'm not talking about **ART**, I'm talking about **FUNCTIONAL DRAWING**.

If you're thinking, "Yes, but do I really have to draw this stuff? Can't I just use image-search tools on my computer?" then I offer you this:

I'm going to give you some of the science, but for me it boils down to one thing: drawing fires up a part of your brain that tapping on a keyboard never will, helping you think and work differently. Oh, and it's also a whole lot more fun, which I guess makes two things...

equipment

You don't need much to work visually, but here are some items that you'll find useful along the way.

- ☐ Felt tips (lots of black ones, but also colours).

- ☐ Chisel tip marker pens. Again, black ones but also some colours are good.

- ☐ Paper. A4 paper, flip chart paper and if you can get your hands on it, some of the big stuff.

- ☐ Sticky notes. Ideally 4 or 5 different colours.

- ☐ Index cards.

- ☐ Stuff to stick with. In my toolkit I have Scotch tape and white tack.

- ☐ Sticky dots, for voting.

- ☐ Washi tape. I find it useful for making connections when I'm working up on the wall with sheets of paper, index cards or sticky notes.

- ☐ A blank-page A5 notebook.

- ☐ A cheap sketchbook. Mine is A3.

If you want a linked kit list, then you can find one at **graphicchange.com**.

you're designed to
be visual

3

why?

the evidence as to why we should all be working more visually is pretty overwhelming

No doubt you've already heard a lot of it, otherwise you wouldn't have bought this book in the first place.

I'm not going to delve too deeply into the science, but I will summarise some of the key reasons why it's worth it. Worth it for you, for your business and for your clients.

You might already feel that you have a preference for visual learning styles, and that some of us have a natural preference for Visual Learning. Now of course, if that sounds like you, then this way of working will appeal to you very strongly, but that is just a tiny part of the story.

you're designed to be visual

Your brain is so clever that it can take in massive quantities of data, decipher it, translate it into a format you can understand and relay it to you in a way that you can make use of. Genius.

You are so well designed you can take in huge amounts of complex information, literally in the blink of an eye. In fact, with most of our sensory receptors being in our eyes, 90% of data is already communicated to us visually.[3]

it's more engaging

Working visually engages more of your brain.[4] Literally. Visuals connect with all four of your brain's lobes: the frontal lobe: emotions, planning, problem solving, concentration and writing skills; your parietal lobe: spatial and visual perception; your occipital lobe: interpreting vision; and your temporal lobe: language, memory and organisation. So more of your brain is engaged when you are looking at visual communications.

it's quicker

Communicating visually works so well that it's not whether your drawings are good enough that you need to worry about, it's that you are using the right visual, in the right place at the right time. In fact, you can process visuals so efficiently that you can absorb more information, more efficiently than in any other way.

try this

If you're not sure whether or not to believe me set aside 15 minutes and try this exercise:

1. Find a magazine.
2. Flick through and pick a photograph of a scene. Any type of scene is fine.
3. What did the photo make you think and feel when you first saw it?
4. Now get into literal mode and write down everything the picture is communicating.

I mean **EVERYTHING**. What can you see, what size are the objects? What are they doing? Are they interacting with each other or with you? Make a note of colour, emotion, feelings, the weather, the lighting, the placement of objects. Be as thorough as you can — I promise I'll only make you do this once!

Did you fill one paragraph? Three? More?? All of that information. That detail and minutiae, those feelings and emotions, the message the photographer wanted to convey...all of that you pretty much picked up in a couple of seconds of looking at the image. You saw it, you interpreted it and you made sense of it.

You can get a sense of a visual scene in less than 1/10 of a second.[5] That is pretty powerful stuff, especially when a study from Microsoft revealed we now have an attention span shorter than a goldfish.[6]

it's more effective

A picture is worth a thousand words. I'm sure you've all heard this saying, and it's true. That's why we already use images when we know communication is critical, urgent, or both. If a manufacturer doesn't want you to drink the liquid because it's poisonous, then writing this in text just isn't going to cut it. You'll have drunk the darn poison before you get through the small print!

In our fast-moving world, we need images that are instantly understandable. That grab our attention, whoever we are and whatever language we speak. Research has shown that it takes just 250 milliseconds for a visual symbol to be processed and understood.[7]

look at the image below, then the word. can you feel how even this simple, single word takes a tiny bit longer to process in your mind?

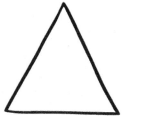

Triangle

it's stickier

You will not only be able to understand information quicker, and remember more of it because it's visual, but you will also be able to remember it for longer.[8] Recent research published in the *Quarterly Journal of Experimental Psychology*, showed a significant recall advantage for words that were drawn instead of written.[9]

It all seems a bit too good to be true, but I promise you it is.

it's more inclusive

Whether you are mainly communicating internally within an organisation, or externally with clients, you can't afford to assume everyone has the same ability to understand, absorb or retain written information.

More than ever before we work globally with people who speak a range of languages. Our potential audience has increased in size and diversity, and knowing that, you can be sure the literacy level of your staff and clients is also hugely varied. Did you know, in the UK over 10% of adults are functionally illiterate,[10] almost 8% of the population has English as a second language[11] and 10% of the population are dyslexic?[12]

The fact is, if you want to communicate effectively, if you want to communicate with the largest number of people, then you need to use visuals.

Kate Power and Kathy Iwanczak Forsyth know this.[13]

They are the authors of a fabulous book called *The Illustrated Guide to Dyslexia and Its Amazing People*.

"For us as dyslexics, conventional books on dyslexia had too many words. So we broke down the key messages into bite-size elements and turned them into visuals to help us share the strengths and challenges of the subject."

Their approach taps in perfectly to the desire for accessible content, so it's no surprise the book became an instant bestseller.

it's helpful

Back in 1982 research was done, which compared a group following a set of instructions with images and another group following the same instructions without images.[14] The group whose instructions contained the images were a massive 323% better at following the instructions. 323%!

it's good for you

And relax. Drawing lowers cortisol (the stress hormone) and strengthens neural pathways, which some believe slows down mental ageing.[15]

if you are taking the time to communicate, make it count

The truth is simple: working visually helps you see things differently, it engages people (including you) and helps your audience focus right where you want them to. Working visually promotes creativity and makes everyday interactions more productive and enjoyable.

Although this way of working has been around for a really long time, (hello...cave people?!) it's still an innovative way of working. This gives you, as a visual worker, a competitive edge.

It gives you a skill not everyone has, but everyone will be impressed with. It can make your meetings and workshops more effective, your presentations more interesting, and keep your documents alive rather than gathering dust on a shelf.

If you want to engage people effectively and make an impact, working visually is the way to go.

It's a powerful tool to have at your fingertips.

If you need any more convincing, let me introduce you to Jen Harvey. As Google's Academy Spaces Strategy Lead, Jen knows something about working creatively and visually in a business setting. As well as heading the Academy site in London, Jen is leading on Google's strategy to develop more dedicated education spaces across the globe. I first met Jen about five years ago when I was drawing at a Google event.

interview with
Jen Harvey

how important do you think creativity is in business?

Creativity is hugely important. Creativity helps us come up with ideas, it makes those ideas even better than they could originally be. It is how businesses set themselves apart, build a USP and strive for success.

how do you use visual thinking approaches in Google, and why?

When we are trying to solve a problem, it's always good to step away from it and break up the elements that are involved. Being a visual thinker myself I always use creative aids (drawings/ diagrams) to visualise these elements. This could be through sitting around a big whiteboard with laptops down or working our way through coloured [sticky] notes.

The Academy team enjoys using the visual approach to communicate our personal brand and our strengths, what our growth areas could be, and what our passions are. Seeing this in a visual format allows me to get a better picture of the person I am working with and how we can work together more effectively.

We've seen an increase in using visual storytelling methods at events — it reminds me of how tapestries were first used to depict an important story in history, so clearly it's something that has proven its value to humankind! We are also including more visual cues in slide decks rather than rows and rows of text.

A simple picture can sometimes say more than a text-heavy slide. Just embellish the story yourself and embrace the role of storyteller rather than script reader.

where's a good place for people to start working visually?

Ideation sessions — sit around a white board and pull a problem apart. If you can, get someone in to draw your findings from a meeting so that you can step back and take a bird's eye view of what happened. Or simply grab some [sticky] notes, get the right people together, move away from the desk and let your creativity flow over that business challenge.

— Jen Harvey
Academy, a Google Space

part

2

**introducing YOU the
visual worker**

4

....

you

i was a child of the 70s and hopeless at sport

I was always last and frequently humiliated. Drawing became my escape. When I was 14 I finally got sick of compulsory cross-country runs, brutal games of hockey and communal showering and I started to boycott PE (Physical Education for those of you who aren't Brits).

Each week on a Thursday afternoon after lunch I would go with the rest of my class to the changing rooms and ask my gym teacher if I could be excused so that I could go and draw.

Drawing was something that I was passionate about, I was good at, and, perhaps most importantly to me, I was able to draw without being humiliated in front of my peers. Each time my request was denied and I was punished, typically by being made to sit in a corridor, or in the changing room doing nothing. This went on for months. Eventually, no doubt despairing at my stubbornness, the school relented, and for my final year I was able to take double art. Two extra blissful hours of drawing each week, and no more short-skirted humiliation.

you might be wondering why 'm
telling you this?

Well, I believe that by using the visual tools in this book your skills will grow, your communications will work to their max and your clients will be more engaged. Your business will perform better than ever before and you will be able to clearly see the benefits of this way of working.

But, to really get the most out of this book you are going to have to get comfortable with the skills involved in working visually, and that includes drawing... that's right, I mean putting real pens to actual paper. I know how, deep down, a lot of you feel about drawing, a bit like I did as a 14-year-old girl each Thursday as I headed to gym class. A sense of dread and a fear of imminent humiliation.

I want to say right now that you have nothing to fear in this book. I will show you everything you need to know to be able to draw and work visually, and although you won't believe me yet, I have never, in well over ten years of training, found someone not able to learn the skills I'm going to share with you. I believe that is because within you, within all of us, is a natural creative.

The fact that you picked up this book makes me know that you are already creative. Creativity is a state of mind, not of artistic talent. Your business might not be in the creative sector, you might have failed art at school, and you might not have crafty hobbies, but the fact that you were drawn to this book means that you are attracted to the notion of working differently, of working creatively, and that is a great jumping-off point.

(Of course, you might already be super confident about working visually, and have bought this book to explore some new tools. In that case, feel free to embellish the drawing exercises in whatever way makes you smile.)

If all this talk about drawing is starting to give you the sweats, don't worry. This is not about being an 'artist' at all, but about functional drawing, and learning simple methods to help you communicate more visually. This book is for you even if you 'can't draw' at all. Really, no artistic talent is necessary.

I know, if you're not a confident artist, hobby sketcher or super crafter, you might be feeling sceptical at this point. You might even be thinking, "Uh oh... I didn't know I'd have to actually draw... I can't!" or "It's easy for you to say I don't need to be artistic Cara, but I **REALLY** can't draw!"

i understand that it can be hard to believe that working visually is for you, but...

one of the best-kept secrets of working visually is that anyone can do it, most people think they can't, and almost everyone will be impressed with you when you do

So suspend your disbelief for now and come on this journey with me.

start by taking a breath

Now let's assess your stress level. Have a think for a moment about how you feel about drawing. Imagine drawing at your desk. Maybe showing someone else something you've drawn... Imagine drawing in a meeting, with the lights on and people looking.

I know, right?!

stress thermometer

Have a look at this stress thermometer and identify how you're feeling.

If you are somewhere near the bottom half of the thermometer that's great. Hopefully your confidence will continue to grow and we will see you out in the world putting your skills into practice straight away.

Now, if you're near the top of the thermometer, don't worry. Read on and let me reassure you.

TERRIFIED

SCARED

NERVOUS

EXCITED

COOL

A lot of adults are a bit terrified of drawing. As young children, we're happy drawing and communicating visually. It's natural and fun. You haven't yet developed any hang ups, in fact you've probably received praise for your efforts.

Then you go to school and within a few years you've been sorted into those who can draw and those who can't. Our art work is graded. Perhaps we 'fail' at art. We hear adults around us say that they can't draw, reinforcing the idea that it's a hard or unusual skill to have.

Even if we don't have our confidence crushed, we are educated to equate text with intelligence and pictures with... well, childishness. By the time we leave education and enter the world of work, it's no wonder the vast majority of communication is written or verbal.

Most of us lose the connection we had as children with being natural visual communicators. To make matters worse, a lot of us will have been taught, quite wrongly, to equate artistic skill with creativity. When we stop seeing ourselves as artistic, we stop seeing ourselves as creative visual individuals.

And that's a serious flaw in our education system, because at the same time, in the world of work we're increasingly being told that we need to be creative thinkers and problem solvers. Innovators. No wonder people are confused. After years of misinformation, it can feel like a massive leap of faith to step back onto the path of creativity and not feel like a fool or an imposter.

Denisse Ariana Pérez, author of *Democratize Creativity* says it well:[16]

"How dare they let us believe that creativity is yet another categorical binary? Some of the most creative people roaming the streets of this world are completely unaware of how creative they actually are."

you are creative

We are all creative. And we need to start a cultural shift where we separate artistic talent from drawing, creating and visual thinking.

Now I know we can't all paint a masterpiece or write a great novel. The people who can do that are exceptional. Rare. But we all have elements of those same skills buried within us. If you doubt that, try asking a group of pre-schoolers to put their hand up if they can draw, or paint, or sing, or dance or... you get my point, they will all put their hand right up.

If you don't have ready access to a group of pre-schoolers, here's an exercise, developed by Bob McKim, Stanford Professor and a pioneer of visual thinking.[17]

creative circles

Look at this page of circles. Grab a pen. Now, how many of the circles can you turn into something else?

Don't worry if the ideas are silly or impossible in the real world. I've done the first one for you. Set yourself a time limit of five minutes and off you go, see how many you can fill in! If you don't want to draw in the book, just draw out a sheet of circles before you begin.

The desire to create, and the pleasure it can bring us, is a deep part of who we are. It is individual and societal reactions that build negative associations with drawing or creativity in our minds and our hearts. This negative conditioning comes from all quarters. Our teachers, our friends and family, the media and of course our own selves. The negativity become internalised as we compare ourselves to famous artists and professional creatives.

And of course, all of that negativity has an impact. It stops us from experimenting, from enjoying creativity just for the sake of it.

I can't tell you the number of times someone has told me that they can't draw. I mean thousands of times. My usual response is to say that, "Yes, yes you can draw well enough, everyone can." The reply to that is typically, "No, you haven't seen my drawings! Really, I can't." The most common place I hear that said is at the beginning of a training session, and so usually within an hour that particular negative inner voice has been silenced. But it's powerful isn't it?

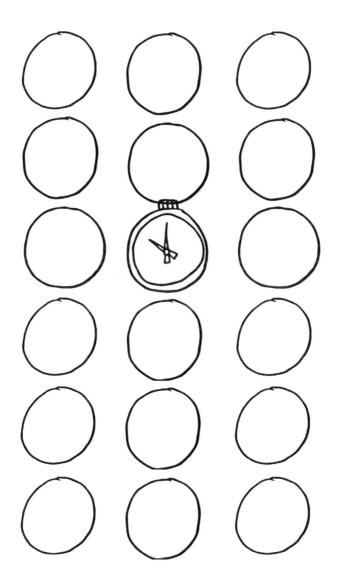

list of doom

Here's a suggestion: on a loose sheet of paper make a list of any negative feelings and thoughts you have about your own creativity.

If it makes you anxious or scared, write that down. If you think your drawings are rubbish, write it down. Sometimes, externalising your inner critic, shining a light on it, can make it easier to stop focusing on that negative voice. Once you've written your list, you can put it aside...

reset to positive

I was at a job a while ago, working with the leadership team of a national utilities company. We had a day of team bonding activities and thought-provoking presentations, all captured in a big graphic record. At the end of the day, one of the senior engineers came over to me and said, "All my life I never thought I was creative until today. I never knew all these different ways of doing things existed, and I've found out that I'm quite good at them. I'm creative!"

Nothing makes me happier than seeing people rediscover their creativity.

To help you make the mental leap from "can't draw" to visual worker try this exercise:

patterns of success

Close your eyes and think about the things you are good at. Now pick one of them. Something that on your mental CV of life you can think... yeah, I'm good at that. They don't need to be 'creative' or work related, in fact they really can be anything.

One of mine would be making soup.

I'm not a great cook by any stretch of the imagination, but I can pull together a tasty soup, out of whatever random ingredients are in the vegetable drawer.

Write your skill on a piece of paper and put it in front of you.

now ask yourself the following questions:

☐ Was there ever a time in your life that you couldn't do this well?

☐ Was there ever a time when you made a mistake?

☐ Was there ever a time that it didn't work out as perfectly as you'd hoped for?

☐ Was there ever a time where you improved your skill level by learning something new?

If you answer is yes to any of these, then take heart. The only difference between this skill and learning to work visually, is that the skill you wrote down is one you already feel confident about. When you feel confident and knowledgeable about something, you're more likely to feel happy jumping in, experimenting and making mistakes.

Conversely, when you feel anxious about something, when you don't feel confident, then those small mistakes, those attempts that don't work out, or even just imagining the things that can go wrong, can make it feel as if you have already failed. It can be easier to say, "This isn't for me", or "I can't do it", than to feel that the mistakes, the learning, the mishaps are actually all part of the experience. The mistakes are what teach you what not to do the next time.

The mishaps and experiments are how you grow in skill and in confidence.

I can think of many soup disasters. Burnt pans when I got distracted. Soup that tasted all kinds of bad because I used too much of the wrong something... the soup that ended up full of pepper when the lid to my pepper pot fell off as just as I was adding the final touch... but did I let any of those disasters stop me making more soup? Nope. Instead I let my knowledge that soup making is something I'm good at carry me forward, and 9 times out of 10 the next soup is delicious.

So, I want you to embrace your nerves, they are a part of learning something new, and not something to be afraid of. Accept that you will make mistakes, and that some exercises might feel harder than others. Know that you can do this, you just don't know how yet, and that is what this book is for. I will share with you everything you need to know, and show you how you can do it, step by step.

Now take the list of negative thoughts that you made. Screw it up and throw it in the bin.

We are going to reset to positive. You're going on a journey and I'll be here to guide you.

You already know that communication can be more interesting, more fun, more engaging and more effective. I know that because you're here. You're already a **VISUAL WORKER** in your heart, you just need the tools and confidence to put it into practice.

so let's get going

let's draw!

5

skills

visual dictionary

To begin, I want you to grab a small notebook that easily fits in your workbag. It doesn't have to be expensive. Ideally it will have blank or grid pages, so that you can draw freely in it. This will become your visual dictionary. Your very own reference tool that you can refer to next time you need to draw something similar, or before you head into a visual session. Here's how it works.

As you work through the exercises, I want you to use A4 or A3 paper so you have plenty of space to practise, make mistakes and perfect. Some of the images you draw, you know you'll want to use again, so I want you to copy these out into your small visual dictionary so you have them handy when you need them.

See an image that you want to figure out how to draw yourself? Put it in your visual dictionary. Next time you need to draw something similar, or before you head into a visual session, flick through your visual dictionary to refresh your memory. The more you fill your visual dictionary, the more images you will have at your fingertips to inspire you when you need them.

let's draw

Over the next few chapters you're going to build up a collection of simple images (icons) that are individual to you and your business. They will be icons that you can use as you work through the toolkit later in the book, and they are icons you will use again and again when you're communicating visually in the future.

I'm going to focus on showing you how to draw some of the most common icons.

You can work with any paper and pen, but typically I use A4 or A3 paper and a black fibre tip pen or felt tip.

it really is this easy

It's always a good idea to start at the beginning, with the basics, don't you agree?

look at these marks

What do you see?

A face, right? These two dots and a curved line are almost impossible to see in any other way. Did it take an artistic genius to draw these? No, of course not. Can you draw them? Yes, of course you can.[18]

If you're thinking, "Okay, I can draw that, but why bother when I can download an emoji...?" I need you to understand that it is the act of drawing rather than the standard of the drawing that is really important. Let me explain why...

Downloading an image and drawing an image are wildly different. The former is a passive activity. You search for someone else's work, look at it and use it.

It's a bit like turning on the TV and watching someone go for a walk.

In contrast, to draw the image yourself... well, that's like putting on your trainers, going for the walk, feeling the breeze on your face and the pavement beneath your feet.

it switches on your brain — it engages you

When you draw something yourself, you have to think, not just about what you want to draw, but what you want to convey. You have to make choices about the mark you make... this long or a bit longer? This colour or that? This deep thinking happens quickly and a lot of it happens unconsciously, but still, because of the power of your visual brain, it embeds the information more deeply, connecting you to the issues more effectively, and allowing your mind to open to the possibility of seeing in a new way. I mean really, it's amazing, and all of that is exactly the same no matter how good (or how basic) your drawing is.

For now, you'll just have to trust me. Drawing is really very good for you.

"but I can't draw at all"

Hmmmm. We're back here again.

lightbulbs

I've spoken to dozens of unconnected people who all said, "I can't draw". I ask them to draw a lightbulb. Not copying anything, just using their imagination. If you look over the page, I think you'll agree, that despite all being totally different, they are all very definitely lightbulbs.

DRAW A BETTER BUSINESS

#dbblightbulb

shapes

These are the basic building blocks of everything you'll be drawing in this book. These are the equivalent of the alphabet in your visual language.

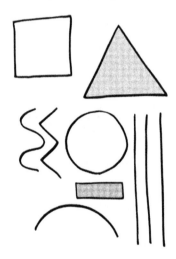

A square. A rectangle. A circle. An arc. A triangle. Straight lines. Wiggly lines. Zig zags.

Have a go at drawing each of these shapes. Pretty easy huh? If you're a self-critic, and I know a lot of us are, then you might be saying to yourself, "oh, my triangle isn't perfect... I can't draw!" For now, just trust me. It's good enough.

If you can already draw well, then you might be saying, "oh this is way too basic for me." So for you, the challenge is to strip back some of your creative stylings and draw images that are super simple and plain.

What you need from a visual is that people recognise what it is, and they recognise it quickly, without having to think about it.

Your drawings need to be:

simple + recognisable

This means they are:

1. easy and quick to draw and

2. easy for your audience to understand. In my world we call these simple images **ICONS**.

Here are two reasons that learning to draw simple icons is useful:

- It gets you comfortable drawing, being creative, and thinking visually in relation to your work.

- Your brain works best when you draw the images yourself. It makes sense to have a set of simple 'go-to' images to call upon when you're drawing something up on the whiteboard, or working stuff out on the back of a napkin.

Think of this like packing your kit bag ready to go and deliver a training session. You make sure you have everything you need right? Double checking you have everything. These simple drawings are some of the tools you'll use to work visually. Practising them now will give you confidence and build muscle memory, so working visually will become easier and more instinctive for you.

buildings

Buildings are all around us. Domestic, commercial and industrial: we live in them, work in them and spend our free time in them. I recently read a quote from designer Ilse Crawford that said we spend 87% of our lives inside buildings! Whether or not that's true, buildings shape our communities and give us a sense of place.

You can see here, some of the buildings that are in my visual dictionary.

Because they're in my own visual dictionary, they are easy for me to remember. Because I draw them often, I can draw them quickly.

What buildings should be in your visual dictionary? Think about the buildings relevant to your world of work and to your clients' world.

Everyone's list will be different, and you can add to it or change it later. Take a moment to write a list of your buildings.

Think about what makes one building look different to another? Sometimes it's the shape of the building, and sometimes it's something you add to a building. For example, a green cross on a shop might make you think of a pharmacy. A coffee cup on a window would make you think of a café.

Don't worry if they don't look the way they do in your head. There's plenty of opportunity to practise. For now, just get used to externalizing what's in your head and getting it captured onto paper.

objects

What objects are important to you and your business? They might be your products and the components that go into them. The objects you use to make something. The objects on your desk, in your toolkit or in your store. The only rule is they need to be an object, a thing, an item that can be touched. So not an abstract concept or idea.

Make a list of the important objects in your business and then, the same as with the buildings, figure out a simple way of drawing each one? Have a practise and then add them to your visual dictionary.

people

People are bound to be an integral part of your business. Whether they're colleagues, customers, clients or part of your supply chain, people matter.

Identify the people important to your business. Write your list, think about the roles people have, and how you might draw them. As with all visual working, there is no right or wrong. It's just a case of trying different things out until you find one you are happy with.

meet Hanna

Hanna runs Riviera Nannies providing the rich and famous of Monaco and the South of France with highly skilled nannies and governesses for their children.[19] Hanna's list of people includes her office assistants, the nannies and governesses and of course the parents and their children.

"I can see how drawing with our staff during training sessions would help us get a fuller idea of who they are, what they do and what they need. I can also imagine introducing visual profiles to our families, a lot of whom have English as their second language, as a way of helping them and their children get to know their new nanny."

This is how simple drawing people can be.

You're bound to make some mistakes but try and have fun. Resist crossing out or throwing away ones you don't think have worked. Learning is about seeing what didn't work so that you can try a different way the next time.

we learn more from our mistakes than our successes

diversity

I believe that there is power in holding the pen, and with power comes responsibility. By drawing diversely, you have the power to make your audience feel included. It can make customers feel your products are just right for them, or a client feel that you're a great fit for their business. It is communication gold dust. I mean really, it's a super power! It builds super fans. It makes loyal clients come back for more. It's a moment of real connection.

But you also have the power to exclude. To make someone in the room feel the dialogue isn't about them, doesn't include them. It's a disconnect. The opposite of what you want to achieve.

Drawing diversely is more inclusive. Fact. And by 'diverse' I mean people who look different from you. Whether that's different genders, skin colour, hairstyle, age, visible impairment, height, size, head coverings... The list could go on and on.

Recently I was drawing at an event and I had just drawn one of my people as a Sikh man with a turban. Well you can guess what happened. A Sikh man wearing a turban walked by and spotted my drawing. He came over and said, "**No one ever draws a Sikh guy!**" He took a photo of the drawing to send to his friends and he hired me, on the spot, for a job a few weeks later.

I can't tell you how many times I see pictures that show only white people, or where all the women look like supermodels, or all the families have two parents, all the couples are straight and all the doctors are men... You get my point. It's a distorted view of the world and it's a sure-fire way to disconnect your audience. So, whatever your own life experience, step outside and mix it up.

If you feel nervous about offending people with your drawings. I offer the following:

As a queer woman, I know how much I appreciate pictures that give a nod to diverse relationships.

Avoid stereotypes, and instead look at real people. So for example, if you don't wear a hijab, or use a wheelchair, make some time to look at pictures, practise and don't be afraid to ask people how you can improve.

Jessica Bellamy

...is an Adobe Creative Resident, an infographic designer and a Design Justice advocate.[20]

"You have an opportunity to use your talents to create and support mindful, authentic narratives featuring unconventional and underrepresented views and faces. Your work shapes perceptions, creates or defines narratives, and designates credibility and authority. It's a powerful tool that we should use consciously and responsibly."

colour

Colour adds interest and vibrancy to your work, and helps your audience focus their eye on the key bits of your communication such as a useful image or a key fact.

The colouring in I'm talking about is actually less like colouring in and more like 'highlighting'. It can be subtle or impactful, it's up to you. I often use quite strong colours like neon orange or shocking pink, because I enjoy the contrast. It really is a personal choice. Colours don't have to be realistic, in fact I rarely use realistic colours for anything.

Grab a couple of different coloured brush or marker pens and look back at the drawing you've done so far. Add in some colour, paying attention to what works the best for you. Remember just a little highlight will do.

connectors

Connectors help your eye travel from one part of an image to another. It's a path for your eye to travel along and will stop your audience from getting distracted and wandering off. It might seem obvious to you in what order someone should look at things, but your audience has no idea what you intended and a random mind of their own... Connectors are a way to lead people gently by the hand on the route you want to take them. Arrows, lines or even footsteps are all types of connectors.

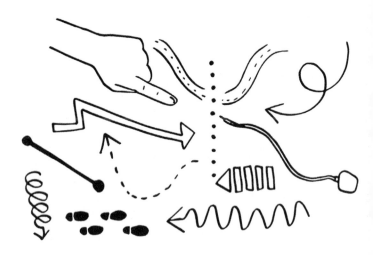

containers

Containers act like a picture frame around sections of content. They keep your audience's eye where you want it. It also tells your audience that all of the information inside the container is connected. A container can be as simple as a square box, or as creative as you like.

learning to communicate visually is a lot like learning any language. it takes a bit of practice

6

....

everyday

you've got the basics in the bag — well done you

The functional drawing skills you've learnt in the last chapter really are everything you need to get going. The rest of working visually is even simpler. If you scored yourself at the nervous end of the thermometer exercise earlier in the book, I hope you've started to feel a bit more confident.

Learning to draw is a bit like learning to play an instrument or run 5 km (though not as good for your waistline!). You follow the instructions and it's tough at first. You practise and it gets easier. Eventually you've got it. You've strengthened the neural pathways and built the muscle memory you need to be able to repeat and continue to improve your skills. **BUT**... you need to keep using your new skills or they will start to fade. The feeling of confidence you have will leave you and you'll find reluctance or nervousness creeping back in when you're presented with an opportunity to work visually.

So how do you prevent that happening? That's right, by building a habit to keep your visual muscles flexed and ready for action.

This a pick 'n' mix selection, so take what you find helpful, and ditch the rest.

doodling

Doodle every day. You already know how to doodle, of course you do. You might not have done it since you used to doodle in the margins of your school books, or you might find yourself doodling every time you find a bit of paper within arm's reach. For those of you who are doodlers, you might already know doodling often happens when you're listening, like when you're sitting in a meeting or listening to someone on the phone. Despite its bad image, doodling doesn't mean you're distracted, or that you're not listening properly. In fact, evidence shows that doodling whilst you listen or think can actually help you focus and process better![21]

A good way to get into a doodling habit is to keep a notepad by your phone or TV and doodle whilst you're taking a call or watching a show. Don't stress about what you're doodling, just allow yourself to make spontaneous marks without editing yourself. (If you like doodling you'll love my interview with super-doodler Sunni Brown on page p178.)

sketchipes

I like to cook and when I have a recipe I love, like my mum's proper Christmas stuffing, I put it into my own handwritten recipe book. Whilst I'm doing it, I add in some little illustrations. It makes the recipe book much nicer to read.

Equally you could draw your shopping list, or what you're going to pack for your holidays... you get the idea, just add in some visuals to any kind of humdrum list.

For some sketchipe inspiration, check out *They Draw & Cook* (theydrawandcook.com) for some online browsing, or if you prefer something real-world, head to the cookery section of your local bookstore and check out *Salt Fat Acid Heat* by Samin Nosrat & Wendy MacNaughton.[22]

SERVE WITH ALL THE TRIMMINGS
BUN, OR IN A PITTA
(IF IT ALL JUST FALLS APART, JUST PUT
EAT... IT'S STILL DELICIOUS!)

sketchnotes

Sketchnotes are a visual note-taking practice that incorporates simple pictures and shapes, along with text to effectively capture content. A sketchnote isn't supposed to replace written minutes where they are necessary, but the reality is that for lots of us the pages of notes we write in meetings are often left unread and are quickly forgotten.

All of the valuable snippets of information you have just gained from your meeting or conference are hard to retain without a memory jogger, so heaps of hard-won information is lost to us. Information that we thought was important enough to take time out of our busy day to hear in the first place... lost.

So it's no coincidence that more people are sketchnoting for themselves than ever before. It can be a really effective replacement or supplement to formal written minutes.

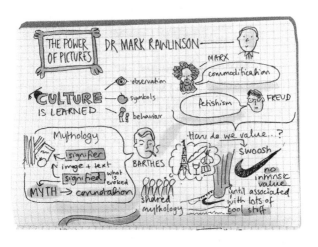

draw sociably

draw with kids

It doesn't matter if they're your kids, your nieces and nephews, or even your neighbour's kids (but then do ask permission first). It's a universal truth that kids love to draw. Take advantage of their positive vibes and settle down to some drawing. They won't judge, and you might even find yourself pulling some impressive moves out of the bag once the pressure of adult scrutiny has been removed from the mix.

Kids are wise beings when it comes to drawing.

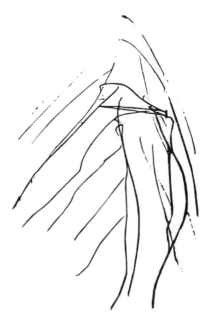

tree Chelsea age 8

Years ago, I was on a two-day train journey in the wilds of Canada. After one stop a small girl sat next to me and noticed I was drawing in my journal. She reached into her backpack, got out some paper and crayons and started drawing too. Great! A fellow appreciator of sketching on the road. She drew a cat and showed it to me. Entering into the spirit of the situation I drew a countryside scene straight from my childhood. Big fat trees, fluffy clouds and a round sun.

"What's that?" she said pointing to my trees. "It's a tree" I said. "No, it's not!" she declared. "That's not a tree!" she said, tapping my picture for emphasis. Feeling a bit hurt that my tree didn't pass muster even with an 8-year-old, I asked her to show me how she would draw a tree. Which she did, and she was, of course, totally right. I kept her drawing, and when I looked out of the window as we crossed the icy tundra of northern Canada I had to agree, her 'tree' definitely looked like the trees I could see, and mine... well mine looked nothing like one at all.

draw with grown-ups

If you don't fancy drawing with kids, then adult drawing clubs are springing up all over the place. Whether you fancy drawing life models in the pub, urban sketching on a Sunday afternoon, or joining a sketchnote group, there are lots of adult options for getting your pens out.

journalling

If you keep a journal or a daily record, try adding some illustrations to support your main points, or to represent your feelings or thoughts.

My journals tend to be a mix of words, drawings and scraps of things that I find to stick in on the way. I do it in part to occupy myself when I'm sitting in a strange place watching the world go by, and partly to help me remember my trip in a way that, for me, is more meaningful than the photos I've taken with my phone. When I look back on these visual and written notes I can transport myself to the place, remember how it felt and what I was doing in a way that nothing else does for me.

Sunday 8h
Walk along the river to Bow Falls which are beautiful. The water is a pale glowing

woman
with man
7·9·02
Parc
Mont Royal

daily exercise

Set yourself a challenge. One of my students, Franziska, asked a colleague to give her two random words every day that she would then have to draw.[23] What a fantastic idea! Alternatively, you could pick a book (any book will do) and draw one line out of it a day... great to get your mind used to interpreting random and sometimes abstract content.

So, you get the idea. In fact, you've probably had some other ideas yourself. It really doesn't matter what you do, just that you find ways to build little bits of simple drawing into your day-to-day life.

sorted

interview with
Eva-Lotta Lamm

illustration by Eva-Lotta Lamm

Eva-Lotta Lamm is a sketchnoter extraordinaire. She produced a beautiful travel journal *Sketchnotes einer Weltreise* (Notes from travelling the world) which is well worth a look. Here's what she has to say about sketchnote journaling:

do you think sketchnoting added to your experience?

Sketchnoting my travel diary made travelling more interesting because I became more interested in the things around me. I started observing things and people more closely because I knew I wanted to sketch them later. I got (even more) curious and observant about small details and paid more attention to everything going on around me.

Sketching regularly served as a way to digest the multitude of new impressions and to have some time for reflection every day. Of course, there were days when I didn't feel like sketching and I struggled to keep up with my diary, but it was usually just the 'getting started' that I struggled with and as soon as I had been sketching for five minutes, I enjoyed it.

Sketching every day made a huge difference to my sketching abilities. Practice is huge for making progress.

what are the benefits over text-only journaling?

I find a mixture of images and words more fun to look at again later. Visuals are very accessible, both on a structural and an emotional level. It's easy to browse the pages and feel like you are back in the situation.

Drawing in public is also often an immediate conversation starter. People got interested when they saw me drawing. I had lots of interesting conversations thanks to my journal.

what would be your advice to someone new to this?

Start small. Take your time. Keep doing it.

You don't have to switch completely from only writing to only drawing in one go. Pick a few moments in your day and add a simple drawing of a thing that reminds you of the situation to your text. If you do this regularly, you'll see that it will get easier and easier to find images to add, that your observation of the things you want to sketch will get sharper and that your pages will eventually get more and more visual.

— Eva-Lotta Lamm

evalotta.net/sketchnotes

part

3

it's a virtuous circle

7

toolkit

drawing inside your business

In **Part 1** I shared with you the value to your business of working visually, and in **Part 2** I showed you some of the basic skills you'll find useful as you get going.

Part 3 contains a series of tools for you to have a play around with and try out.

I will give you examples to copy, and a bit of narrative about why I think you should use the tool, but this isn't meant to be prescriptive. If the tools you create look different to mine that's great! If you can see how to use a tool in a different type of situation, brilliant!

Use my examples as inspiration but don't feel tied to them, they are just a jumping off point. You can change the headings, change the shape or change the pictures, in fact change it all! This section is designed to show you variety, so that you can create your own business pick 'n' mix of visual methods that work for you.

The more you work in this way, the more you build those neural pathways and feed your creative visual brain, then the more this way of working will become second nature to you. It's a virtuous circle.

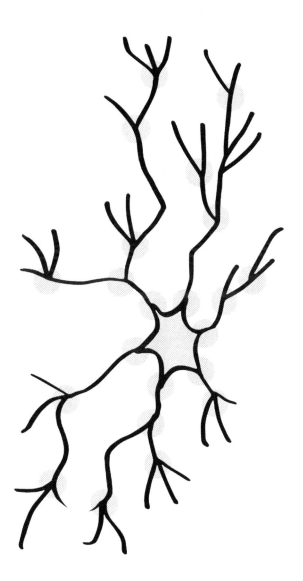

planning that comes
from a place of
creativity

8

plan

plan

When you run your own small business it's all about you. It is shaped by you, nurtured by you, and ultimately will stand or fall because of the choices you make.

That's a lot of responsibility. It can be lonely, scary, fun and exhausting.

One of the downsides of carrying all this responsibility is that you are busy... and I mean really, really busy... most of the time, right? As a small business you might be juggling delivery with development, with marketing.

You can be so busy focusing on ticking off your epic to-do list, earning enough, getting the next client, that before you know it, you can't remember the last time you stopped and turned your attention back to the big picture. The big plan.

This section of the book is about **PLANNING YOUR BUSINESS**.

There are lots of reasons we need to plan. Whether that's for the next meeting, a big move, or to kickstart the next challenge. Sometimes we get stuck and making a plan can help us to see a way forward. Sometimes we lack clarity or lose sight of our goals and a good plan can give us the stepping stones to follow that will keep us on track.

This is not the planning of scribbled to do lists or productivity apps. They have their place, but I'm guessing you're already doing some of that.

This is a pick 'n' mix of planning tools that harnesses more of your brain and more of your imagination simply because you're doing it visually. This is planning to better understand your business. Planning that saves time and promotes alignment. Planning that comes from a place of creativity and imagination rather than dread, and that will help you reconnect with your big dream, giving you tangible steps to help you get there.

let's plan

planning track

I was once in the senior management team of an organisation. I was responsible for six departments, each with its own manager, budget and team. When I started the job, I found each department was operating as an island, with none of them having a connection to, or an understanding of, the central drivers they needed to be operating within.

If they didn't get their completed project plans to me, they couldn't get their plans signed off. If their plans weren't signed off, they couldn't accurately budget. If they didn't have an accurate budget, key items would be missed and the fallout from that... well that would last all year.

To try to align my disparate teams, I created a visual planning tool that revealed the cyclical nature of the system they were working in. I called it the Planning Track because it reminded me of a race track in shape. It works both as a calendar or deadline prompt sheet, and as an overview of the big picture.

It's pretty self-explanatory and can be used to equally good effect if you work on your own but want a simple tool to keep all your key events in mind, and in one place.

It worked really well with my team. The managers felt less isolated, and I had a great tool to keep everyone, including me, accountable.

Have a look at my example here. The headings and drawings can be whatever is meaningful for you. You can colour in the track as each month passes, you can add in dates, or leave it broad as I've done.

Of course, if you get into planning tracks like this you can also have one for a month, or a week, or even a day!

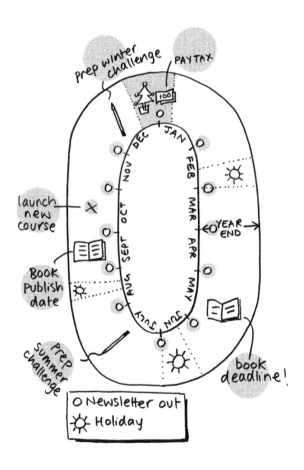

mind maps

You might be familiar with mind maps, but when did you last use one?[24]

When I came to start this book I was overwhelmed. It's my first book, and there is a lot of planning involved. I mean a **LOT**. I felt stuck before I'd even begun. Then I remembered mind mapping, and (drumroll please...) ta dah! The planning process was back on track.

The drawing of a mind map is a visual tool that helps you reach conclusions and identify connections. It is a creative act that triggers creative thinking.

So here's the lowdown on how to mind map like a champ. There's no rule book, but generally, working with your paper in landscape gives your ideas more room to spread and to grow.

Look at my example. You can see I've used words and pictures. (This is a good time to use some of the icons you learned in the last section.) I've also used some shapes and lines to help me navigate the flow.

Let your mind map wander following branches of thought to new conclusions, helping you have ideas and make connections in a way that writing a list, or thinking in your head just can't do.

I ended up with a total of 130 nodes on my book plan! A pretty effective way of unlocking brain freeze.

pick a
habit

refine

exercises

PRACTICE

READ
this book

exercises

?what
do I need
first

capture
results

improve

DO

SHARE

ID
clients
it will
benefit

practice
+
refine

get
feedback

sticky planners

method #1

I also used sticky notes as a key tool in helping me to plan this book. I began with a mind map, but once I had the bones of it mapped out, I used sticky notes to refine my plan. Firstly each section heading had a sticky note. Then each chapter was added. I used different colours for each section so that I could instantly see if the balance was feeling right or not. Of course it evolved once I started writing, but here is the first sticky planner for my book.

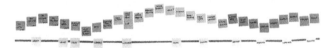

Index cards are also a great way to refine a plan.

When I was further into the detail of the book content, I wrote each chapter on a piece of paper and laid them out on a big dining table so I could move them around and further fine-tune the order.

method #2

Here is a super-simple sticky-note planner that taps beautifully into your visual thinking brain. You can find lots of inspiration for tools like this on Pinterest.

On an A4 sheet draw a simple template with a space for six sticky notes, and space for Today's Goal. Then simply write out a goal for each day of the week and stick them on a pre-created template.

Each new day move the goal to the **TODAY** box. When you've done, put it in the bin. At the beginning of each week your sheet should be empty and you can start again.

easy

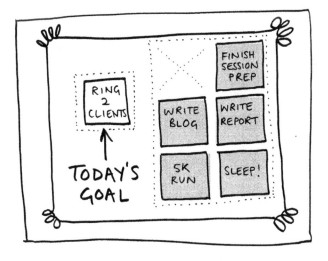

method #3

As someone running a small business, I have a lot of plates to spin. Take this week's projects for instance:

1. Blog to write.

2. Client-facing delivery day.

3. Admin to do (emails, travel bookings, quotes, invoices).

4. Social Media to maintain.

5. Support students on two of our online courses.

6. Write next chapter of book.

7. New course to develop.

8. Create downloads for newsletter signups.

Now some things have to happen. They are core day-to-day work. But some tasks are big. Really big. They're projects, really.

These bigger tasks take thoughtfulness, careful planning and creation time. They are often a bit of a risk, without a known return on investment, making them hard to prioritise when you know the other stuff has got to be done.

Now you might wonder what the problem really is. I mean if you're busy delivering and keeping the wheel turning, shouldn't that take priority?

My answer to that is, "not always".

I think there is a big problem with letting the business-as-usual activities bully the projects to the back of the queue. It is often those big, thoughtful, time-consuming projects that have the potential to be the real game-changers for your business, and in the long term, ultimately the big money makers.

So here is a quick sticky-note solution that I use to keep the big projects rolling. It's a simple mash-up of the first two methods.

Sticky-note each of your big projects with a chronological task list.

Take the sticky-note containing the very next step from any (or if you're feeling ambitious, all) of your big projects, and move that sticky-note to somewhere you won't miss it. This could be adding it to your weekly to do list, sticking it on your computer or on your fridge. Wherever will keep it front of mind. I like to stick mine on my mouse mat!

This is helpful in two ways. Firstly it makes you break down your big projects into small steps (one sticky-note each), and secondly, by separating the next step from the big list, it helps you focus on the next step. Of course you might choose to take that one sticky-note and then type it into your calendar or productivity app, and that's okay. Its main function has been achieved already.

gap mapping

It's easy to think, when you've been running your business for a while, that you're clear on what resources you've got, and that you have a mental shopping list of the things you need.

In part it's probably true, but often what we put on our mental shopping list is either the next step up from what we have, or just what we want in a particular moment. Neither of those things are necessarily what your business needs.

This tool helps you look at resources in relation to your desired business future, helping you map out the gaps.[25]

The first step is to draw up your template and identify your resource bundles. For example, people, tech, equipment, knowledge... Grab some sheets of A4 paper and draw one template for each bundle. One per sheet.

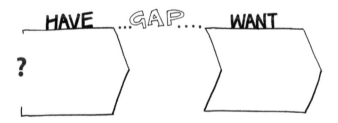

Now think about what you want your business to look, feel and be like? For your business to get there, what do you need each of your resource bundles to look like? Capture those on the right.

This is your **WANT** list.

Now head to the left. What resources do you **HAVE**? Right now, where you are? (Note, we start with the **WANT** list so that you don't limit your thinking based on what you **HAVE**).

That leaves you with the blank space in the middle. This is your resource **GAP**.

So, if I take my people bundle as an example, I want a network of skilled individuals that work with us on the projects they can excel at, helping us deliver high quality services to our growing customer base.

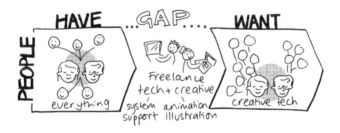

At the moment we are an in-house duo working with a small network of graphic recording, design and film making freelancers.

Our gap is for people who can help us with the technical capacity of the business, as well as specific creative needs such as animation.

It might seem obvious, but capturing your gaps allows you to expand your thinking and identify details such as size or cost, and that puts you in a position where you can start prioritizing. Use the space left on the sheet to have a conversation, or some focused contemplation about what that gap would take to fill.

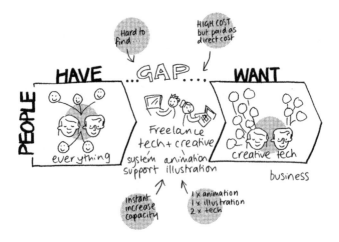

three steps

This is a deceptively simple three step tool that I use in lots of different ways when working with colleagues and clients. I once shared this tool at a training session I was running at Google. When I was invited back to deliver the session again, the Programme Lead told me that it was this tool that she'd used again and again since that first session.

version #1

The three boxes are lined up horizontally, left to right. For your visual brain, this reinforces the fact that we are going to be looking towards the future.

The first box contains the dilemma, challenge or situation. Seeing yourself and your challenge on the page is really powerful. It helps you focus on the issue, and if you're doing this with a client, lets them know you're focussed on that issue with them.

The second box is for identifying key issues to help you gain clarity. Turning a big problem into something with solutions.

The third box is for solutions. Seeing them makes them possible.

The real power of this type of tool is the three simple boxes that take you on a journey from challenge to solution. If you're doing this with a client it enhances the dialogue you are already having by adding an extra level of clarity, focus and accountability.

version #2

You can also use the three steps as a review tool, useful whether your project was a great success or totally failed. At the end of the steps write the outcome of the project, so for example 'Booked for repeat session', then work your way backwards. What are three key steps you took to bring that outcome about? Can you identify actions you took that made a difference? Put them in boxes 1 to 3 in the order they happened, to help you reflect.

simple, eh?

trail map (the big plan)

On a warm Wednesday one summer, I attended a conference. I'm sure you can picture the scene: a big hotel, a stuffy conference room with little natural light and a lot of beige décor. It was after lunch and I was starting to feel tired when the facilitator said, "I have a visual tool called a **PATH** we can have a go at if anyone's interested?"

And that is how I ended up spending the afternoon being trained in a planning method called a **PATH** by one of its creators, Jack Pearpoint.[26] I was so inspired, that a small group of us worked on into the evening, hunkered down in a side room, getting familiar with the method.

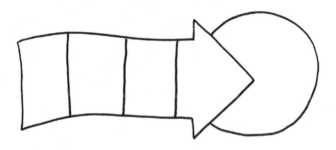

Since that day I've helped to deliver many **PATHs** and have seen what an effective tool it is. Over the years I've tweaked the **PATH** that I was taught, taking some elements, and adding others, into a tool that you can use on your own business. I call it the **TRAIL MAP**.

This is a hefty five-part tool. Each section is useful in its own right, but when you add them together, it is really powerful.

You will:

- clarify or reconnect with your dream

- identify tangible focused goals

- identify key elements you need in place to reach that goal

- construct a detailed action plan to get you there

This might seem daunting. I mean, the reason a lot of small businesses don't have a business plan is that it can feel like too big a task when there are so many other things to do, right? But it is worth it.

Amy Nolan runs an online business called Ginger Rainbow designing colouring in gifts for children. "My biggest weakness is that I come up with plans and lists, put them aside and then go back to making things up as I go along," Amy told me. "The Trail Map broke things down, helped me focus and, if I got stuck or distracted with another shiny new idea, it helped me stay on track. It's now part of my routine to look at it every day."

A couple of months ago Amy emailed me to let me know that one of her big dreams, to have a range of greetings cards published, has just come true. Marvellous!

If you're running your business alone, then this plan is your friend. There to guide you and lead you back to the trail when you go astray.

If you have a team, the **TRAIL MAP** will ensure you're all on the same trail, moving forward together with shared goals. Really, it's good stuff.

So here are the five stages of the **TRAIL MAP**:

1. Dream
2. Focus
3. Resource
4. Action
5. Reflect

If you want to complete it all in one go It will probably take 2 — 3 hours. Alternatively, you might want to pause in-between stages. You can use a flip chart or sheets of A3 or A4 paper. I'll show you in each section.

right then, it's time to get started.

trail map 1 — dream

Now I believe that visioning, the act of imagining and drawing the future, of sticking a pin in life's map where you want to be in a year, or five years, can help bring clarity to your ambition, and it is this clarity that can help you realise your dreams more quickly.

One day, back in 2005, whilst having a coffee with a good friend, I did just that. I drew, on the back of a napkin, my dream. I wanted my own business, earning my living creatively. I wanted to earn enough to replace my salary, and I wanted the freedom to work with varied people, and projects.

Now at this time I was a manager in an NGO and in no way an artist. I'd never owned a business and I had bills to pay. I'd been fantasising about having my own business for a while, but this was the first time I'd actually sat down and put some energy into visualising my dream.

Now I'm not saying that visualising your dream is magic. You still have to put in the same amount of hard work to make it happen, but I believe that articulating your dream, and capturing it visually, makes the next step of looking at how to make it happen much more likely. It might seem too simple to be serious, but trust me, using visual tools is powerful stuff.

My first little dream on the back of a napkin got me going, in fact within one year I'd started my business.

you will need:

- Time away from phones, emails, and demands of family life, so schedule it in. Allow at least one hour for this
- A sheet of paper
- A black felt tip or marker pen, and some coloured pens, too

In the centre of the paper draw yourself. Now it doesn't need to be fit for the National Portrait Gallery... just a face or a person that represents you to **YOU**.

On the top right-hand position of the page draw a star, or another positive image that resonates with you and write the word **DREAM**. We put the dream star in the top right-hand corner because it is both in front of you (forward-facing) and slightly above you (aspirational + positive).

now it's time to dream...

Although you might not think it, this is the really hard bit. In fact, the majority of adults struggle to dream big. (When I say big I really mean **BIG**.) That's because most adults have lived a long time with limits. Whether they were set by you or by others, these limits start to shrink what you believe to be possible, and that, my friend, is a sure-fire way to achieve less.

Note: You're not dreaming big enough if you have already started the things in your dream!

Imagine the perfect version of your business in a world with no limitations. Money is no problem, time is plentiful, you have all the help you need, and there's no end to what you can achieve.

You can own a private jet, you can have a million followers.

If you hate networking, no worries, just dream you have the perfect little black book, bulging with A-list clients.

If you're wondering, "why bother if those things can't be true?" then I want you to trust me for now. As you get further along the **TRAIL** you will see how your big dream is an essential foundation for everything that follows.

Take as long as you need, relax your mind and imagine... What is your dream business? What does it look like? What is it doing? Who for? How? Try and identify the different elements of it. Give it some solidity, imagine it right there in front of you. Try and make the images in your mind as detailed as possible.

Now as you dream, a thought you really like will appear in your head. Great! Now stop for a minute and draw an image or a little scene that represents that element of your dream. You can add key words too alongside your pictures. Add detail, if it's red, colour it in, if it has a bell and whistle and a handle on it, draw them all. Capture the detail of the dream. Got it?

Right, now you just need to dream, draw, repeat.

dream, draw, repeat

It can take a while. Fill your page. When you think you've run out of dreams, dig deep and push on, asking yourself different questions. Get it all out and onto your **DREAM** page.

Thinking creatively in this way stimulates you to have ideas you hadn't considered before, and this is a key element of making your business innovative. So, expand your mind as wide as possible. Stretch your dream as far as you can, because what you are really doing, with each stretch, is removing the limits from what you might achieve.

My first big dream had me drawing in the sunshine in the garden, I had published books, I was running courses around the world, drawing in amazing places for exciting clients, being an expert and (strangely?!) owning a red van to put my equipment in. All of these things (apart from the red van!) I've now achieved, but back then, before I even knew my business could work, before I'd had a single paid client, before I'd had any success at all, this was well and truly dreaming big.

trail map 2 — focus

Dreams are great. Essential, in fact. But the very measure of a good dream — that it is huge, fantastical and maybe even a bit wild — is what makes the focus stage necessary. You now need to convert the wildness into something that you can implement, here in the real world, where there are budgets, limited hours in the day, and the basic laws of physics apply.

Now this isn't to put a damper on all that stretchy thinking. It's important it stays there just as big and bold as ever, as without it your business really will never achieve all that it is capable of. Let me give you an example:

Westglade Primary School in Nottingham, England, works hard to give an amazing education experience to children who live in a challenging city district. They're a staff team that are good at dreaming, and one of their dreams was for the school to be in a wildlife park, to take classes with lions wandering the playground. Just think of what the children could learn if that was their environment? It would be amazing, right? Great, so I promptly drew a lion and some trees onto the dream picture.

Now clearly this wasn't going to be achievable in reality (we're talking about lions + children here...), but it sparked a discussion. What might be possible? Some animals that wouldn't eat children? Still sounds good, eh? So then we focused on what was positive and possible. I drew some trees and a goat.

One year later we revisited the plan. What had become of the dream? Well, the school had been awarded a grant. They had set aside a section of the playing field and begun turning it into a wildlife adventure area. There were trees and tall grasses, logs to climb on, and they had even made a home for some chickens.

gorgeous

So you need to take your dream and focus in on what is **POSITIVE** and what is **POSSIBLE**.

That last point is important. It's easy to focus on the positive. On what you want, wish and hope for. But if it isn't possible because of some earthly constraint beyond your control, it's not worth your focus.

Alternatively, it might be very possible, easy even, but if it isn't positive, then again, it's really not something you want to spend your time pursuing. So, **POSITIVE** and **POSSIBLE** is what we're looking for.

Grab another piece of paper, or if you are doing this as a group then you might want to scale up and have an even bigger sheet than the last.

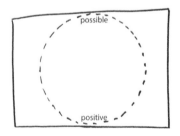

Draw a circle filling the page, and on the edge of the circle, write **POSITIVE** and **POSSIBLE**.

Now this is the really important part. I want you to go back to your **DREAM** sheet. Pick an element of your dream. Look at that image and ask yourself the following question: What could this look like in reality, in one year's time?

A year is a good timescale because it's a big enough chunk of time to really make some changes in your business.

Now the key to this exercise is to keep the heart and the purpose of the idea intact. Here is an example of what I mean:

Remember the example of the wildlife park becoming a wildlife adventure area of the playground? The lion became the goat, and eventually became a chicken!? The heart of the idea was to bring nature to the children. The purpose was to use this as an experiential learning tool. The chickens achieved that just as well as a lion.

So, taking each of your **DREAM** elements, apply the focus. Ask yourself what's **POSITIVE** and **POSSIBLE** and draw this new focused idea into the circle.

Don't forget to keep your drawings simple. They are there to help you focus, not as full-on works of art. Once you've filled in your circle, you have your list of business goals for the next year.

trail map 3 — resource

Now let's move on to the resources you'll need in place to carry out your **POSITIVES** and **POSSIBLES**.

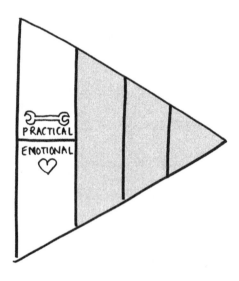

You'll need this template to be quite big, so if you have a sheet of flipchart paper. This is your **ACTION** Triangle, and the section we are looking at first is the left-hand column, **RESOURCES**.

You can see this column is split into two sections. One space is for you to look at **PRACTICAL RESOURCES** and the other space is for emotional resources, i.e. emotional support.

Starting in the **PRACTICAL** space, I want you to write all the different practical resources you will need to deliver your list of goals. Look back at the **POSITIVE** and **POSSIBLE** circle and think about each goal in turn. Be specific. Do you need training? A particular object or tool?

Meet Emma, Jeanne and Beth, who run a business hub.[27] Outside their building is a courtyard and their dream was for this to be a sanctuary for busy city workers. They wanted a community garden and to host a monthly makers' market. When they focused in on this goal, the practical resources they identified were:

- ☐ market stalls
- ☐ a licence to hold a market

As you write each practical resource onto the sheet you're also creating a future to-do list, so it's important to be clear and use words that will still mean something to you in the weeks and months to come.

Now, take the emotional support box and repeat the exercise. What emotional resources will you need in place to deliver this next stage of your business? Do you need time set aside each week to reflect? Do you need to identify someone who can check in with you each month to see how you're doing?

There is no right or wrong. It's just a case of thinking about what **YOU** need to be the best you can be.

trail map 4 — action

This is the last big section. Set aside about 30 minutes for this.

You've got your one-year goals in place in your **POSITIVE** and **POSSIBLE** circle. This next section is for you to think six months ahead.

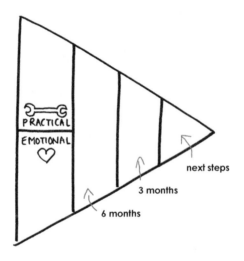

Take each goal in turn. Think about where you'll be in six months' time for that individual part of the plan. If it was a quick win you might have completed it, or you might be just about to start.

Once you've thought about where you'll be up to with each particular goal, write it in the template. And repeat.

Remember Emma, Jeanne and Beth who wanted to have a community garden? So for six months' time their list looked like this:

- ☐ gardening group in place
- ☐ raised beds constructed
- ☐ planting underway

Moving on to the next box, do the exercise again, now asking yourself: to have achieved all that in six months' time, where should I be in three months? Repeat the process taking each action in turn.

Emma, Jeanne and Beth had their six-month goals for the courtyard garden. Their three-month list looked like this:

- ☐ gardening group identified
- ☐ materials for constructing raised beds donated

Finally, you have one piece of your **ACTION** Triangle remaining.

I want you to think of what your next steps will need to be. By next steps I mean something tiny you can do in the next seven days, like find a phone number or put something in your diary.

By taking this first tiny step you have made everything possible.

trail map 5 — reflect

So you've done it! Well almost. Firstly, you need to piece together all your sections.

Find a big table, floor or wall space and lay it out like this:

If you've got the space to display it as a whole, then I recommend taping the pieces together and displaying your whole plan up on the wall.

Now you might notice that it looks a little bit precarious at the minute. A bit like a balancing game, trying to see if you can get your **ACTION** Triangle to stay up by itself. This is a lot like running a business. Even when you've made the big effort to come up with a plan, it can be easy to get distracted and it can all collapse.

So, there is one final step I want you to take; I want you to add some stability.

I want you to think of positive words that describe how you feel about your new plan. How you feel about your business evolving.

Think of at least four separate words (but as many as you want) and write them on the big sheet that you used for your **ACTION** Triangle like this:

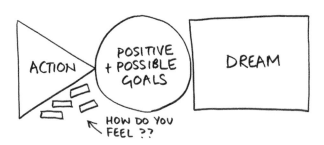

These words are the wedges that keep everything in place. When you're losing focus several months down the line. When something goes wrong and you start to feel things aren't possible. When life or bills or.... you get my meaning... when stuff happens and everything starts to feel a bit wobbly. Then revisit those words. Let them give you strength and use them to refocus and reconnect with your **TRAIL MAP**.

"if i can't see it or smell it
i won't buy it"

Ruby Wax

9

engage

If you want to cultivate your business, to have it grow, whether that's in size or turnover, or both, then you have to give as much attention to how you engage as you do to how you deliver. In this chapter we will look at how you can think and behave differently. Making more meaningful connections that will draw clients to you, create loyalty, grow super fans, increase your income, and ultimately make your business the best version of itself.

In this chapter you're going to look at your clients and think about who they are, and you're going to follow them on their journey through your business so that you can tweak, fine tune and finesse your offer.

Stopping to dig down into your business like this can feel counter-intuitive. Of course you understand the logic of it in principle, but it can feel an awful lot like standing still and navel gazing, rather than doing the do, delivering and earning money.

This, though, is the truth:

if you don't understand, you can't engage
if you don't engage, you won't sell

I have a website, and I use social media, but in my 12 years of running a business I've never spent any additional money on marketing or advertising. And yet, I have a steady stream of job enquiries and quote requests landing in my inbox each month.

Now as much as I think I'm excellent at what I do, I put most of that incoming stream of enquiries down to the fact that my work is visual, it sticks in people's minds, and when they're looking for someone to work on a particular type of project, my images are there, front and centre, ready to give them a nudge.

Contrary to what it might feel like, spending this time increasing your understanding and ability to engage, is not standing still at all. In fact, it's more like building than digging. Building a staircase that will take you and your business up to the next level.

each insight you gain is another step

ideal client

Branding guru Bernadette Jiwa says that

"the biggest mistake a brand can make is to try being all things to everyone. Weak brands settle for doing what's easy or obvious. They appeal to the market of everyone, avoid the edges and thus become interchangeable with their competitors. Strong brands know they are this and not that. They intentionally aspire to be something to someone and so become irreplaceable to their customers."[28]

When I started my business, I hadn't given much thought as to who my Someone was. Don't get me wrong, I had a notion of who I thought would buy my services, but I hadn't really thought beyond that. I was of course missing a fundamental element of engagement with this half-hearted approach. Let's face it, without clients, you really don't have much of a business at all.

method #1

The purpose of knowing **WHO** your ideal client is, is to be able to engage with them more effectively. But just knowing who your ideal client is, is only part of the exercise. You also need to understand **WHAT** their dreams are, and **WHAT** problems they have that need solving. This is called Empathy Mapping, a phrase coined by Dave Gray[29] founder of XPLANE and a leader in the world of working visually.

You can find a downloadable PDF of XPLANE's empathy map on their site (link at the back of the book). It's a thoroughly good tool and I've used it a lot. But I want to give you a couple of alternative approaches.

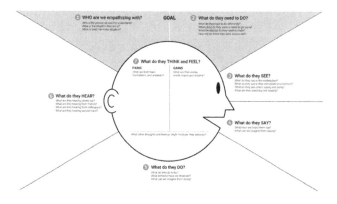

method #2

Debbie runs a digital marketing business, Debbie Dooodah.[30] When she starts working with a client, one of the first things she does is help them to identify who their ideal client is.

"You need to know who you are selling to and what their problems are before you create marketing content."

Debbie favours collage. Big paper, big pens, some glue and a lot of magazines to cut up. To try this, draw a person in the middle of your page and then build up a picture by sticking on key words and images that resonate with your ideal customers.

method #3

I like to draw visual prompts to get my mind pondering (of course you can add in any categories you like). If you're doing this as a team, work big and write your thoughts straight on. Mentally walkthrough your customer's day and use the visual prompts to trigger thoughts.

Now your ideal client's might be a fiction, but I suggest you make use of any real analytics you have to inform the picture. If you know your best clients are 70% female, aged between 30–45, it might make sense for your ideal client to be from that demographic. If you're wanting to shift your client base, then do this exercise twice. Once with who your customer is now, and again for your desired customer. Seeing them both in front of you will make it easier to start sketching a path between the two.

To try this approach, write a list of the areas you want to explore (as you can see, mine was: Think, hear, say, dream, love, value, but you can add in any categories you like). Once you've created the visual prompts, sit with your picture and mentally walk through your customer's day, taking notes as you go.

advantage cycle

Once you've given some good thought to who you want your clients to be, then you're in a good position to start considering how you attract them to your business. This tool will help you identify key values to engage with your audience on. Great to do before you begin your next round of marketing activity.[31]

The advantage cycle goes something like this:

Pretty much common sense, right?

I'm going to take it as fact that you're really great at what you do. But...

I'm sure you've already realised, that being great at what you do is not enough to make your business succeed. Talented people fail in business all the time. Hopefully this tool will help.

let's start at the top

You're great at what you do. Check!

You know there are potential clients out there with a need your business can fill. Check!

Now... unless you address the next step in the cycle, there's a risk your potential new customers might buy from someone else. If they do, they'll never have the great experience of your product, and so never recommend you to their friends...

This is the key bit of the cycle. If you get this bit right, the cycle carries on turning and your customer base will grow.

Think about your clients and what is most important to them about your product or service. Is it the ingredients? Is it the cost? Do they need to be able to get it ASAP? Try and identify four Value Points.

For this tool we're going to go back to visual basics, with some graphs. Draw a cross and label each arm with one of the value points.

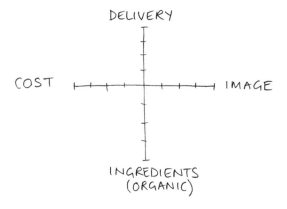

Write a list of everything that makes your product or service exceptionally good. What experience, knowledge or skill do you have that elevates you? What do you offer that stands out from the crowd?

Let's imagine you make a luxury beauty product.

- Maybe your product appeared in a magazine.

- You might have 20 years' experience, or been trained by a renowned expert.

- Maybe you've won an award.

- Your product might be the most luxurious in its cost bracket.

- Or you might have ingredients that are all 100% certified organic.

Once you've identified what makes you brilliant I want you to plot them against your client's values. (The centre of the grid is something you're not doing. The outside point is something you're doing brilliantly.)

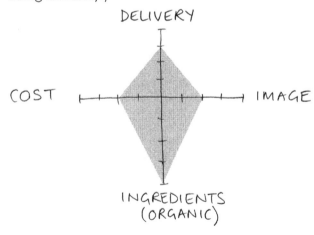

Your brilliance and your client's value points might not be a perfect fit, so think creatively about how to connect them. Your product might be sourced from local ingredients with no air miles. This isn't the same as being organic (which in the example is a customer value point) but, it speaks to similar ethical values, so I'd include it on that arm of the grid.

Now it's important you don't get sucked into your own hype when you do this exercise. Be really honest with yourself about how you're doing. Finally, join up the dots to easily see both the areas you're strong in and those you might need to pay a bit of attention to.

Okay. Now repeat this for your two main competitors. Use a different colour, for each, so you don't get confused answers. My recommendation is to use pale colours that are a bit transparent so you can see through one to the other. If you don't have any, then you could use a different chart for each.

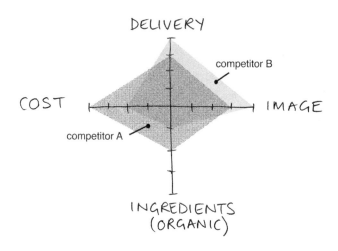

finally let's look at them with your graph laid on top

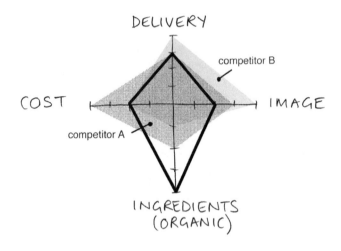

With competitor A you can see that their image is better and they have a better cost point. For competitor B they have better delivery and image than you. **BUT** you have better ingredients than either of them.

THAT is your advantage.

It's easy to focus on your weak points. **BUT** I say, do the opposite. Spend your time and your marketing budget shouting about the things **YOU** excel at and let your competitors chase you. Alternatively, use your insights to identify opportunities to collaborate.

focus groups

Over the last 25 years I have helped deliver a **LOT** of focus groups. From back in my social worker days when I co-led a consultancy specialising in engaging with hard-to-reach groups such as children in the criminal justice system all the way up to today, where I set up a beta reader group for the development of this book. Whatever the subject, the one thing these sessions all had in common was visuals.

here are a few ways to use visual thinking tools in a focus group setting:

capture

This takes two people, one to lead the discussion and one to capture the content into a pre-created template. So, for example, when working with Macmillan Cancer Charity on a focus group session, I captured the answers visually from each key question being asked on a big sheet of paper at the front of the room.

Participants could see their views were heard and valued, and during breaks they could come over and connect with the visuals. The visuals were then scanned and shared with the group at the end of the session.

generate

Working at a session with a TV network, looking at consumer ideas for Saturday-night TV shows, the session began as a big brainstorm. Each idea was quickly (and roughly) sketched up onto an A4 sheet and put up on the wall. In less than an hour we had about 50 new unfiltered ideas.

We were then able to group the initial ideas into themes and use these new groupings as a jumping off point for the next stage of the discussion, creating further iterations of these core ideas.

vote

Once you've got all the thoughts and ideas out of your heads and onto paper that everyone can see, you can imagine how it's now quite easy to vote or prioritise the content. A quick way of doing this is to use sticky dots. Just give everyone three dots to stick onto their favourite ideas and see which gets the most. Of course, you have to be conscious of herd mentality with public voting, but it's a quick way to get a snapshot of people's preferences.

You can also use sticky notes or index cards. Getting people to physically line up their order of preference, externalising their thinking, helps the decision-making process as the participant can clearly see the impact of each change.

customer journey

Marie was a consultant living in Paris who took part in one of my workshops. A round trip of 850 miles. During the morning we struck up a conversation. "I wish," Marie said, "that you offered this in Paris…" Now Marie wasn't the first person to say this. I'd had many individuals ask me to train in their city or country. And I have worked with organisations and teams all over the world, but the logistics involved in running a workshop open to the public are challenging, and anyway, I was already too busy. Right?

The day after the workshop, I gave myself the gift of an hour to sit down and ponder the question of Marie.

Marie wasn't the first person to travel from mainland Europe for training. In fact when I looked at the workshop data, people were regularly travelling big distances. Of course, that level of commitment is wonderful. People coming all that way to be trained by me… Woohoo! I must be doing something really right eh?

Except when I sat still long enough to contemplate it from their perspective, when I travelled along their customer journey, I was actually doing pretty badly. There were hours of computer research, travel time, days away from home and additional costs for Marie. Not great.

In fact, when I add the next layer of a customer journey, the emotion, onto the page it looks something like this:

- [ ] Want to be trained in working visually – excited
- [ ] Search for courses and find Cara's website — excited / frustrated
- [ ] Book course — excited
- [ ] Research travel and hotel options – frustrated
- [ ] Book travel and hotel — relieved
- [ ] Travel to course — excited / anxious / tired
- [ ] Do course — excited / tired
- [ ] Travel home from course — really, really tired

It was this realisation that led me to explore how to offer my training online. I had been so focused on making the destination high quality, I hadn't stopped to consider the journey to get there.

Ideally you'll have a nice long piece of paper to do this exercise. To begin draw a long horizontal line. This is the line your 'customer' is going to journey along. On this line, plot every touchpoint your customer has with you or your service.

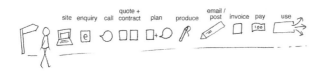

Now go back along that journey and try think about how your customer might be feeling, and draw an emoji at each point. If you've got data on this, great. When do customers drop off the journey? When do you get the most questions or complaints? Of course there's no substitute for asking your customers, so consider putting out a survey or running a focus group.

At the end of my customer journey I am often asked if I have suggestions as to the best way to share the visual output into the wider organisation.

This gives me an obvious place to look at how I can improve my customer's journey. Once you've addressed the obvious, continue on to interrogate each of the touchpoints in turn, asking yourself (and your customers) how you could do better.

service blueprint

When I have an idea I can be impatient, keen to get on and put it into action. Which is, you know, energetic, lean and dynamic and all that, but really prone to mistakes. A service blueprint is a great way to ensure changes are made where they're going to be most effective.[32]

Joy and Paul set up Bit + Blade, supplying a small but essential machine component to large packaging companies.[33] In their first year they had steady growth, but things had then levelled off and they were struggling to see what could be changed to increase orders. After all, the component part could not be made to wear out any quicker, despite wishful thinking!

I suggested doing a service blueprint and one afternoon in April they came to our studio.

Again, a big sheet of paper is great for this exercise, or you can stick together some flipchart sheets.

The service blueprint begins with the customer journey that you've already completed. Then underneath that journey you're going to add new layers of insight. So for Joy and Paul we added: a row for the customer's thoughts, a row for what they were feeling, what actions took place at each touchpoint, and what system was used to support or generate each action. We then looked at any negative interactions or emotions and devised a plan to improve the experience.

The most useful way I've heard this process described is to compare it to a theatre.[34] Front of stage is where all the public interactions take place. On the stage are your customers and sometimes you or your staff... the customer journey is the performance. Backstage is where the mechanics happen, where interactions are taking place that the customer doesn't see. There you'll also find the props, the scripts... these are the systems that you are using.

Service designer Paul Moran describes it as "end to end plus detail" and he's noticed the benefits:[35]

"Having a single common understanding on the wall in front of you, makes it much easier to have useful conversations about different elements of the journey. Teams quickly begin to see how everything connects and has an impact on the experience a customer has when they use the product or service."

Let's get back to Joy and Paul... At the end of our April afternoon, they had identified two points in their service blueprint where they could make changes for the benefit of their clients, in the hope that this would stimulate sales:

1. They could change the threshold at which free postage kicked in.

2. They could be more explicit on their website about the provenance of their components, which are not the cheap, mass-produced imports of their competitors, but are crafted in Germany to an exceptionally high standard.

Having made the changes, Joy reported back a couple of months later with some good news.

"Working through everything visually was really helpful to us. We made some simple changes and started to see an increase in sales and new customers really quickly."

great result

**interview with
Sunni Brown**

how did you get into working visually and eventually writing *The Doodle Revolution?*

I didn't want a normal job. I wasn't a person who could function in a normal job. So as soon as I saw this work, at the Grove,[36] I thought, oh, this is the perfect integration of a lot of the things that I knew how to do, I just had to teach myself how to draw a little better. I already knew how to listen, how to pull out what was meaningful and relevant.

So as a practitioner I began working visually, group problem solving, designing agendas, moving people through group processes, and I ended up doing that all over the world. That was when I noticed how reticent people were to draw. No matter where you go, people are freaked out by the idea of drawing, and they apologise for themselves and they're kind of ashamed. And I was like, wow. There was something really off about our understanding of visual language. And it was universal. So writing *Doodle Revolution* was me throwing down the gauntlet.

how do you work visually inside your business?

In my business I never try anything without seeing it first. If me and my team members need to have a meeting, I will draw what I'm going to talk about and send that to them first, to accelerate communication. Or, if I'm designing an agenda then that's always done using images in a sequence, I can share that sequence, and kick -start the conversation right away.

any advice for someone new to this way of working with clients?

If you're new to this and unsure about how to integrate visual thinking with your clients, don't ask permission. I would start with something non-intimidating. Have a structure that is not overly imaginative, or cartoon-like, or hyper-visual. Just something familiar to them, something they can anchor to that is not alienating.

So, if I wanted them to do a project map of the steps required to complete something, I would have a big grid drawn on the wall when they walk in. I'd say, "Here's what we're doing."

Who doesn't know what a grid is? And then, you can start drawing, start adding arrows and circles, and comments. Start with a structure that is familiar and go from there. In other words, don't start too deep, too fast.

do you meet a lot of scepticism from clients?

I'm respectful of people's scepticism about working visually, because I was like that, too. When I first encountered it, I was thought, "Oh, these California weirdos." You know?

So if a client is sceptical I say, "Well, why don't we try it?" It kind of sells itself once people actually see it. It accelerates everything, it engages people at a much higher level. It allows for the possibility of new insight. It gets all your mental models externalized.

If somebody still said no, in my mind, that was not my problem. I was like, "Well, come back to me... I'm from the future, come back to me when you're ready."

I was very, very, confident about its ability to change things. So, I never felt like I was selling something that wasn't true, and that mattered. I believe in it.

People are always talking to each other but seeing completely different things. When you externalize that, you alleviate the problem right away. And obviously, because it's visual, you get archives of your conversations, allowing people to feel heard. I mean, it's just huge.

— Sunni Brown

www.sunnibrown.com

working visually
engages people in a
way no other form of
communication can

10

deliver

The game-changing power of working visually really hit home. For me, it was one day about ten years ago when I was hired by a City Council to discover the stories of children from 'hard to reach' groups, such as children affected by domestic violence. Using all our connections my colleague and I found 100 children who agreed to talk to us, tell us their stories and help shape the future service provision in the city. For several weeks we criss-crossed the city, meeting with small groups of children.

Of course, you won't be surprised to know that we worked visually. These are children we're talking about, right? We used pictures to explain our purpose, find out their concerns, and capture their views. After we'd finished we used a picture to send them the results.

We'd been asked to write a report of our findings for the Board. Now these were senior, serious people responsible for hundreds of services and the wellbeing of thousands of children and their families, who used those services. So we put our serious hats on and we wrote the report. 50 pages or so of words, bar charts and tables. But before we handed in the report we did two small but critical things.

You remember I said we'd collated all the children's views onto one feedback picture? FIrstly we made that picture the front cover of the report. Secondly, we packaged up a big picture on which the children had all added their feelings, and we gave it to the Big Boss.

Now the report was well received, everyone was engaged by the visual summary, and the project came to a successful close. I moved on to other commissions and put those few weeks the previous winter from my mind, until about a year later when I happened to find myself in the office of the same Big Boss. Taking up most of the wall behind her desk was the big picture we'd given her all that time ago. When asked why she still displayed it, she said, **"Seeing those children's stories reminds me every day why I'm here."**

Working visually engages people in a way no other form of communication can. It has the power to tell stories and embed messages people can both understand and connect deeply with. I don't imagine the Big Boss could have said where the written report we'd produced a year ago was. (That's not a criticism — just consider how many reports pass before the eyes of every senior business person a year? Some of them might even be the result of your hard work.)

But, and here's the important bit, the stories of those individual children remained real and present in her office every day, influencing her thinking and reminding her why she did the job she did.

That is the power of visual content. I can't tell you how often I hear from clients weeks, months and even years after working with them, that the visuals we left them with are still up on their walls. It's a powerfully sticky way of working.

So believe me when I tell you: visuals help you deliver content to your clients. Whether you're running workshops, coaching others, working as a consultant or selling a product online, visuals can, and do, make the difference.

agendas

I'm going to start this **DELIVERY** section with a tool that's useful if you run meetings.

Think about an average agenda. Typically they're pretty brief, typed up on an A4 piece of paper and often all but forgotten once the meeting has begun.

A **VISUAL AGENDA** is the opposite of this. It's big, bold and stays on the wall visible whilst the meeting takes place. If you're wondering why it's at all a thing, here are some of the benefits:

1. It acts as a creative and positive welcome to the meeting

2. It creates an initial focus point and sets a tone of creative thinking

3. It helps the session stay on task

4. It can be used as a collaborative collation tool

A **VISUAL AGENDA** needs to achieve just two things to be effective: it needs to tell the audience what is going to happen, and in what order.

Now it helps to think of an agenda as a journey that includes important human elements like a welcome, and when lunch will be appearing.

Each item on your **VISUAL AGENDA** should have an **ICON** that represents the relevant point. When you're choosing an **ICON**, don't over-complicate it. Think about what you're going to be asking people to do in that section, as well as the topic.

So for example, on paper, a point on my agenda, might read like this:

10:30: Discuss and agree new format of team meetings.

What I want people to **DO** is 'discuss the topic'. So I could use an **ICON** that represents either a team meeting, or a discussion.

Work your way down your list, drawing a simple icon for each point. Personally, I'd lay it out in rough first, before doing it on a big sheet to put on the wall.

To make your agenda work even harder, use the agenda sheet itself as a collation tool and get the participants to put their ideas up onto the agenda, using sticky notes.

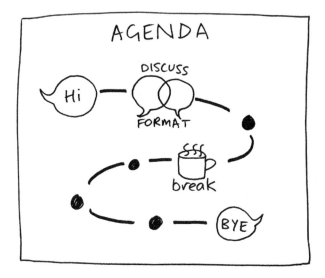

flipchart hacker
hack 1: framing

Flipcharts are used in most workplaces, but they're often used ineffectively. When you begin to use your flipcharts visually, you will see the difference it will make in your meetings almost immediately.

The first flipchart hack is probably the simplest visual trick I can think of. But I swear to you it makes a difference. In fact, a senior business consultant I was working with told me how surprised she was the first time she used it.

"People behaved differently as soon as they walked into the session. One person said, 'this must be important,' another said, 'oh this looks interesting'. Small things, but it meant they were engaged and interested before I'd said a word. I've used it often since and get the same reactions again and again. It still surprises me."

So what is this magic trick, I hear you shout!

It's nothing more complicated than putting a thick border around your flip chart page, and writing a neat, bold heading. It takes about 15 seconds to do.

I use a bumper thick chisel-tip marker in black to make the most impact.

(If you don't have one, it's worth the investment. You should be able to pick one up for about a fiver.) Try it. At the very least it will make your flipcharts look a bit more purposeful.

hack 2: flow

When you use a flipchart, typically it's on a flipchart stand. You write all over one sheet and then you flip it over the top and start on the next sheet, right?

For me this doesn't work. It doesn't work at all. Once the page is turned, the info is lost. In fact, it's worse than that, because what you've done is create a cognitive load for your audience, who will try and retain that information whilst focusing on the new content being added. Here's the solution: instead of turning the page, tear it off and tack it up.

Use the flow of the pages across the wall to enhance the group's engagement, helping them to follow the line of the conversation visually and keep the 'big picture' in mind. Make the flipchart an active part of the conversation.

Now I know that not everyone has a big blank wall to do this with, but I've worked this way on windows, along the edge of desks and taped onto cupboard doors.

Failing those options, just lay it out on a big table top for people to walk along and interact with. Creating a flow of your content helps people approach the conversation with a more expansive mindset, helping you to use it more like a flowchart and less like a deep hole to drop content into. Simple.

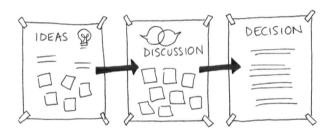

hack 3: parking places

Okay, here is the third hack. I call these one-sheet tools my Parking Places. One image, one sheet but a whole lot of usefulness. Tack them up on the wall at the start of your session and use them to collate contributions (on sticky notes if you want to re-use) that you don't want to lose but that are actually off-topic, or that contain input which could derail your flow if you don't deal with it in some way.

Here are two Parking Places that I use the most often, but I'm sure you can think of a load more.

List the types of meetings you have, and from experience brainstorm the types of side issues that often come up. Can you create a simple sheet to capture them on next time?

hack 4:
flipchart template

Finally, this is a full-on reworking of a traditional approach to using flipcharts, potentially ending the days of sad, dusty rolls of paper shoved under someone's desk waiting to be typed up.

This turns the flipchart from an ineffective (and sometimes illegible) record of comments into a visual framework that will focus and drive your meeting.

Look at the picture on the next page. You can see that I've used simple icons: A lightbulb and an arrow. As a facilitator I knew I wanted the team to:

1. Come up with suggestions to improve our team meetings

2. Discuss the suggestions

3. Agree a way forward

I picked icons that fitted the activity we were undertaking, in this instance the lightbulb (for ideas) and an arrow to symbolize 'action'.

I drew the shapes big enough so that I could write in them and still have room for participants to add up their thoughts on sticky notes. The three ideas we wanted to take forward were added to the action arrow shape.

It looks pretty different to a 'typical' flipchart output doesn't it? Clear and impactful, but allowing you to capture plenty of content. It keeps contributions visible, which helps participants feel valued and stay focused.

Finally, it makes agreed outputs really clear to the whole group.

At the end of this session I took a photo of the flipchart and forwarded it to the participants.

This way of working, of creating visual frames to capture your content into, is widely known as graphic templates.[37] I've even delivered whole-day workshops working from one giant template before. It's a really effective way of facilitating. Let me give you an example of the impact a good template can have.

In a previous job, I delivered a strategic planning session to a team. I created a big template for the session which we worked our way through together. It was a tough session; they were facing a lot of change and feeling demotivated. By the end of the session the team stood back and reviewed their work. Out of the muddle we had a clear, easy-to-see plan. Not in the manager's notebook or on a pile of illegible flipchart pages, but on the wall, in full colour, where it could be viewed by the people that had created it together. On that big sheet of paper, the challenges were acknowledged, differing viewpoints were valued, defined steps were followed and the team were engaged and motivated. I left them gathered and talking around the template.

Now, fast-forward six months. I'm in town with my wife when I get a tap on the shoulder. It's someone who'd been in that session all those months ago.

"You might not remember me, but you delivered a workshop for us," the guy enthuses.

"It's still up in our staff room... can you come and run a session at a public meeting we're having next month?" Now I'm a good facilitator, but I know it was the visuals that had stuck with him.

I did go and draw at that public meeting, in fact it was my very first gig as Graphic Change, because it was that chance encounter at the shops that made me decide the time to set up my business was right now.

storytelling

Telling an authentic story and telling it well is one of the surest ways to connect with your audience. A good story, one that has impact and really lands a hook into people, is one that your audience can visualise.

In business, we tell stories all the time. Stories about what we do, and why we do it. Stories that make your audience feel something or want to buy something. Stories that illustrate a process. Whatever the reason behind your story, visuals bring your story to life and help it connect.

If you can do this well, your story will resonate deeply with your audience, making the ordinary extraordinary and building a bridge from your world to theirs.

Here are four ways you can support your storytelling with visuals.

"there is power and magic –
real magic – in visualising
and telling your story"
Bobette Buster

storytelling: presentations

Presentations are a necessary evil. A boring presentation can sink your good idea like a stone, but a good presentation is a form of storytelling: engaging, compelling and memorable.

A big part of a successful presentation is visual. The visuals of your presentation can either enhance your words and engage your audience, or they can switch off the attention of the very people you want to impress and stop them hearing what you're saying.

Kirsty Mac is a Glaswegian Business Consultant working with senior leaders in large corporations from the finance, beauty and sport sectors. She's also a brilliant presenter:

"I'm doing presentations all the time, whether It's presenting to 1400 people at Wembley Arena, or ten executives on a team retreat in a Scottish Castle. I think business in general is still attached to Powerpoint, so that's the tool I use, but typically my slides are all images. When I'm delivering the presentation I'm not wedded to the words, but to bringing the visuals alive for the audience. The images spark curiosity in the audience, and if you can make someone curious, it's like the top of their head opens up so that more information can go in.

If I'm presenting in a workshop environment then the presentation goes beyond what's on the slides, it's also the materials around the room and on the walls that create visual anchors for the conversations

we're having. I then use the same visual anchors throughout the programme so that people have something to link back to further down the line.

It makes the content stick, which makes it more useable, which helps my clients get a greater return on their investment. Ultimately this is great for my business as they can see the value I bring to their bottom line."[38]

So when you're planning your next presentation, think about what story you want to tell, and spend some time thinking about what pictures will spark curiosity in your audience and connect to the story you are sharing with them.

Here are some tips:

- Draw your own if you're feeling confident — they don't need to be works of art to be effective.

- Hire a photographer. Plan ahead: come up with a list of images, and plan how each 'scene' will work in advance so that you get the most out of the session.

- Use a stock-photo provider like Shutterstock.[39] There are lots out there. There will be a small fee, but it is cheaper than hiring a photographer.

- Don't lift a photo off the internet without the owner's permission.

- Make your images diverse (see diversity, p93).

storytelling:
visual spotlights

Adding a relevant image to your written content helps your audience focus on key words or actions. It's a bit like <u>underlining</u> or making text **bold**.

For example, at the start of this chapter I used this sentence:

If you can do this well, your story will resonate deeply with your audience, making the ordinary extraordinary and building a bridge from your world to theirs.

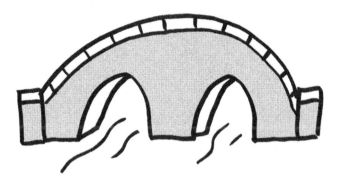

For me the key word in that sentence is **bridge**. If I add an image of a bridge to that sentence, the reader's brain will visualize moving from one side of that bridge to another. Not consciously — it will happen in a millisecond, but it will happen, and that embeds the point I'm trying to make much more deeply than words alone.

storytelling: visual journeys

It can be really effective to pick out the key milestones of your story and show them connected along a visual 'path'. This will help your audience remember those important steps long after your immediate interaction with them is over.

You remember Bobette Buster, the storytelling guru who I mentioned at the start of this section?[2] Well Bobette wrote a book called *Do Story – how to tell your story so the world listens*. When I read the book I also drew a visual journey of the ten key lessons she shares to help embed them in my memory:

storytelling: pitching

One of the biggest tests of whether you're a successful storyteller is whether you're winning at pitches.

Back in 2003, Texan Mary Baird-Wilcock founded The Simplifiers, a company that has evolved from an award-winning events management firm into a successful coaching business, and she has used visuals to help her win pitches from the start.[40]

"In pitch meetings, we lead our clients through our event design framework, telling the story visually of what their attendees will experience from start to finish, and demonstrating how we can help them. You see lightbulbs flip on. They get excited at the possibilities of their next event because they can now see it in their mind's eye. It's such a powerful tool that always helps us win clients. It shows we go the extra mile and differentiates us from our competitors."

Now, drawing in a pitch isn't for most people, so feel free to pre-create. (This is my name for doing the drawing ahead of the meeting.)

I took this approach with a successful PR company who wanted a visual prop for a big pitch. The pre-created visual showed a visual journey of how they work with clients at different stages of the process. At the end of the pitch, they left the visual with the client as an impactful memory hook.

Of course, they won the pitch.

the first time you try this it takes some courage, but the results speak for themselves

infographics

Infographics are, of course, a form of storytelling using data. But I think they deserve their own section. Whatever business you're in, you almost certainly have data. Data that can trigger thoughts or explain ideas.

Good infographics help you show context, comparison and pattern in a way that is revelatory and which, in turn, can help your clients and your business.

You probably already know that an infographic gets way more shares and likes on social media than text-only content, but a vaguely relevant picture stuck next to some text does not an infographic make. A good infographic adds to your audience's ability to understand, connect with and think about the information being created. In the words of David McCandless, the infographic provides "cognitive assistance".[41]

I've met David McCandless a couple of times, (if you haven't seen his book *Information is Beautiful* then I'd really recommend it – it really is beautiful) and I love his view that good infographics are often born out of problems, boredom or ignorance. Using your clients' challenges or problems is a great place to start when you're considering what information is worth putting into an infographic. Apply just a bit of research, or imagination, and boom! You're not only creating engaging, interesting and shareable content, but you're also being helpful!

source: Levie, & Lentz (1982). Effects of text illustrations.

if you follow instructions with visuals you're 323% more likely to succeed

A good infographic helps the audience understand and connect with information more deeply. If you can communicate why someone needs your service, or what makes it so effective or wonderful, then that just might give you the edge.

Think about what your clients don't know about your products: What problem do they want to solve? Write a list of your answers. You now have a great starting place of issues where an infographic might be valuable.

The best advice David gave to me about creating infographics was to...

"just have fun and play"

So, with that in mind, here is a quick guide to creating an infographic, but expect to have to play around with it for a while.

Don't stress if it takes a few attempts to look how you want it to. After all, a good infographic lasts for as long as the data is current, so it's worth spending the time to get it right.

1. Identify something you want to translate into an infographic. Don't forget this is about giving your audience something worthwhile. Be clear on your goal from the beginning. What do you want your audience to know or understand?

2. Research. Gather the data and make a note of your sources (always include your sources on the end result).

3. Decide what type of metric suits. Do you want to show context, a comparison, a pattern? Use colour, shape, hierarchy, a theme and typography to add clarity.

4. Now the intended use of your infographic will dictate how accurate your ratios and images need to be. Try and be accurate, but don't obsess. To engage with your customers or clients; it might be more impactful to be funny than it is to be millimetre-accurate. If you're hand drawing, cut yourself some slack.

5. Share, share, share.

scales

I love using scales. They are super useful to help people identify progress, movement, success or intention. If you haven't used a scale before, let me explain:

A scale is a measuring tool, just like a ruler. It can measure anything, but I most frequently use it to measure confidence gained during training, with participants being asked to mark their level of confidence with a sticky note at the start of the course, and then again at the end. My aim is to see people move up the scale towards **CONFIDENT.**

As the trainer this simple exercise does some really useful things for me:

- [ ] It gets people up out of their seats and talking to each other
- [ ] It gets them thinking about, and focused on the topic
- [ ] It quickly shows me how people are feeling

As well as being useful to me, it's also a good way to embed a feeling of increased confidence for the participants.

Now of course, in this simple format it's not exactly scientific, but you could assign numbers to the scale to more accurately map improvement. Useful stuff, especially if you're needing to evidence the impact or value of the learning.

That's not all. As well as a way to capture data, visual scales can also be used as change enablers. Some time ago I did some work with a group of offenders. In the session we used a visual scale that ranged from **JAIL** to **CRIME FREE**. Then we asked them to imagine being just one step closer to crime free. A shift of just one step can feel much more achievable.

A visual scale is a powerful tool to help individuals or teams consider change. If you're a coach, or anyone who delivers workshops, I'm sure you can think of lots of ways you can apply scales to your delivery.

visual thinking skills and tools will elevate your business

11

conclusion

conclusion

You've made it to the end, and it's been some journey. I hope you've learned something new, and added to your toolkit. Of course I really hope you are feeling inspired to start working visually across your business, and I'd love love love to hear how you get on.

Yes, I'm feeling a bit AWESOME

I wrote this book because I believe that using visual thinking skills and tools will elevate your business.

I know that small-business owners and entrepreneurs are expert at meeting challenges with creativity and resourcefulness, but it can be hard to prioritise your own skills and professional development. It can be too easy to get trapped in the delivery cycle. But, as we've seen, the brave amongst you who do embrace new skills and techniques can get some impressive results.

As the number of small businesses continues to grow at a pace it would have been hard to imagine ten years ago, we need every business advantage we can get to perform on an increasingly global stage alongside big business clients and competitors.

Writing a book is a new thing for me. It's been exciting, exhausting and terrifying in equal measure. I know that for some of you working visually might feel just the same, and when you start bringing this new way of communicating to your clients, some of them will feel it too.

But once you've engaged your visual thinking brain, once you've experienced the difference it can make and the benefits it can bring, it's an undeniable force. You can't unknow it, and you'll never work quite the same again. In fact, how you see and interact with the world will be fundamentally changed forever.

So visual thinkers unite! Uncap your marker pens, stride forward and draw yourself a path to the next level.

draw a better business

references

1. World Economic Forum, The Future of Jobs (2016)

2. Find Bobette at bobettebuster.com and buy her book Do Story from thedobook.co, Amazon and Audible.com.

3. E. N. Merieb & K. Hoehn, Human Anatomy & Physiology 7th Edition (2007)

4. Mayfield Clinic

5. H. Semetko & M. Scammell The SAGE Handbook of Political Communication (2012)

6. Consumer Insights, Microsoft Canada, Attention spans (2015)

7. P. Holcomb & J. Grainger, 'On the Time Course of Visual Word Recognition' in Journal of Cognitive Neuroscience, 18(10), 1631–1643 (2006)

8. P. M. Lester, Syntactic Theory of Visual Communication (2006)

9. J. Wammes, M. Meade & M. Fernandes, 'The drawing effect: Evidence for reliable and robust memory benefits in free recall' in Quarterly Journal of Experimental Psychology, 69(9): 1752–1776 (2016)

10. LiteracyTrust.org.uk (2017)

11. Office for National Statistics (2011)

12. British Dyslexia Association (2017)

13. amazingdyslexic.com

14. W. Levie & R. Lentz, Effects of Text Illustration (1982)

15. G. Kaimal, K. Ray & J. Muniz, 'Reduction of Cortisol Levels and Participants' Responses Following Art Making' in Journal of the American Art Therapy Association, 33 (2), 74–80 (2016)

16. denisseariana.com

17. This exercise came from Bob McKim who at Stanford University began working on human-centred design and visual thinking back in the 1960s.

18. I came across this example in Understanding Comics, a brilliant book by Scott McCloud – scottmccloud.com

19. rivieranannies.fr

20. jessicabellamy.design

21. J. Andrade, 'What does doodling do?' in Applied Cognitive Psychology, 24(1), 100–106 (2009)

22. S. Nosrat & W. MacNaughton, Salt Fat Acid Heat (2017)

23. panther-concepts.de

24. tonybuzan.com

25. This was inspired by the resource-based view of managerial framework

26. inclusion.com

27. thinkinng.org

28. thestoryoftelling.com

29. xplaner.com

30. debbiedooodah.co.uk

31. This exercise was inspired by an exercise in a great book by Cummins and Angwin, Strategy Builder (2015). They in turn were inspired by Slack, The Manufacturing Advantage (1991).

32. A term first coined by G. Lynn Shostack, in the Harvard Business Review in 1984.

33. bitandblade.co.uk

34. M. E. Miller and E. Flowers, The difference between a journey map and a service blueprint (2016)

35. @pjmoran

36. grove.com

37. David Sibbet pioneered the use of graphic templates and the field of visual organisational consulting

38. kirstymac.co.uk

39. shutterstock.com

40. thesimplifiers.com

41. D. McCandless, Information is Beautiful (2012) davidmccandless.com

thanks :)

Thanks aplenty are called for in the writing of any book and this one is no different.

Thanks to my wife Natasha for her love, patience and endless support.

I had the good fortune to be born to parents who encouraged both creativity and entrepreneurial pursuits. So, thanks to my mum Ann and my dad Ray, who although he is not here to read this would have been ridiculously proud.

Thanks to Alison Jones and her talented team at **practicalinspiration.com**.

Thanks to designer Alex Hardwick. Her skills with layout design and her ability to wrangle InDesign to do her will are amazing – **lineanddotcreative.com**.

Thanks to Ju Hayes for being part of so many of my drawing adventures, Bec Evans from Prolifiko for the accountability and all my beta readers and testers for their feedback and encouragement. Check them out:

Amy Nolan – gingerrainbow.co.uk
Debbie Clarke – debbiedooodah.co.uk
Rachel Hinton – theboogieuk.com
Mary Baird-Wilcock – thesimplifiers.com
Jeanne Booth – thinkinng.org
Sam Appa – samappaphotography.co.uk
Emma Torrance – thinkinng.org
Camelia Geary – cameliagearytranslations.eu
Ros Horsley – rosproofreader.co.uk
Hilary Wellington – ginnysgoodyarn.co.uk
Alexa Mottram - motties.co.uk

Printed in Great Britain
by Amazon